Copyright Notice

No part of this book may be reproduced or transmitted in any form whatsoever, electronic, or mechanical, including photocopying, recording, or by any information storage or retrieval system without expressed written, dated and signed permission from the author. All copyrights are reserved.

Max Lane

Can I Ask You a Quick Favor?

If you like this book, I would greatly appreciate if you could leave an honest review on Amazon.

The Ultimate Guide to Make Money Online:

Build a Passive Income Fortune with Kindle Publishing, Amazon FBA, Affiliate Marketing, Dropshipping, YouTube, Udemy, Blogging, Shopify and much more

Max Lane

How You Can Go From Zero To $1,000/Month In The Next 30 Days...

https://www.subscribepage.com/makemoneyonline1

Make Money Online: Twelve Proven Methods To Earn Passive Income And Work From Anywhere in the World

Max Lane

From Minimum Wage To Financial Freedom Online

I'm Max Lane and I was born and raised in Boston. I dropped out of college and literally was three months away from graduation but I was working online on the side. I actually chose to dropout of college in order to burn the boats so to speak and then pursue entrepreneurship full-time. At the start this didn't exactly work out as planned so I took a customer service support job to finance my life.

I worked for three years in an organization with over one thousand employees and hated the job. For any of you that have a call center background of tech support or customer service support then you know that it can be pretty grueling because your talking all day and since it's a minimum-wage job you have no time. Your lucky to have off Christmas Day. As far as breaks, you're policed about going to the bathroom you know you better be sitting there and holding it. Basically it's just a very controlled environment. Customers are very rude you're getting chewed out by them day in and day out. They're angry and you can't say anything back to them. I was always having to resolve their problems and bosses treat you very much as an expendable. I'm sure that you guys know all too well about how you're not appreciated at all with most lower wage jobs.

I came to the realization that you can lose your nine-to-five jobs at any time. You can face any pain throughout your life because you are depending on a source of income which is not your own. It's the source of income related to someone else and you are depending on it, exchanging your time for money. Coming and doing your best efforts but then you will not get the loyalty from the company to keep you. They can decide to let you go at any point of time if they want to. This and hating my job motivated me to spend all my free time learning about making money online and investing my hard earned wages into learning and starting out.

Now three years later I've been able to do a lot of cool stuff. I made five thousand dollars in a single week and have been very happy to make a legitimate source of income online that has made me independent from the nine-to-five jobs.

You might be thinking that it's not possible for you. You tried, you failed, your not smart enough or you're too old. These are all excuses that hold you back. It's never too late for anybody who is suffering from his or her nine-to-five jobs to think about a legitimate business opportunity that they can start to make money online with.

Ask yourself. Why do you want to make money online? Is it so that you can have the freedom to go do cool stuff, spend more time with family, go travel, go on vacations, not have to work a nine to five job? Or is it to make some extra pocket money?

Whatever your reasons are, if you have reached the point where you are ready to start a new chapter in your life and make money online then read on.

Kindle Publishing - How To Profit With E-Books

Kindle publishing is still one of the easiest ways to start building an online business, especially if you don't have much tech skills. If your a relative newbie to online business and internet marketing then this is a great business model to learn. It's got a fairly fast learning curve compared to a lot of other businesses out there and it's not as complex. It's also great if you don't have that much money to invest. The reason why Kindle publishing is great is because you're leveraging Amazon which has hundreds of millions of customers at your disposal. Amazon still remains as the number one book retailer in the world and ebooks aren't going away. So when you understand the right strategy then that's what's going to allow you to consistently make money long term. This can be a transformational income stream for you.

Once you understand the Amazon search engine algorithms then you can tap into that. Then your also leveraging yourself because you don't have to write the books yourself. You can if you want or you can hire writers ghost writers to write the content for you. Then you can operate more as a publishing company where you're the one that's publishing the book and doing the marketing for it. In the same way, you might also leverage yourself by hiring a graphic designer to design the cover for your book. You can leverage a lot of the process and you can do it in a very inexpensive way.

The most important thing to consider when you're publishing a book on Amazon is the niche or market that you're publishing the book in. Oftentimes a lot of people make the mistake of thinking they have this amazing idea, that they want to write a book on and they spent all this time creating it. Then when they finally put it out there they find that it just does not sell. You can't try to reinvent the wheel or create a new market from scratch. You have got to identify what people are searching for, what's hot and what's making good money. There are ways that you can research that and see how well certain books are selling.

First you have to identify demand and research what's selling on Amazon. Amazon is one of the biggest search engines in the world. People go there and type in a keyword. They might type in, weight loss, or meditation, or law of attraction, or motivation, or whatever it might be. To give you ideas of a niche. Ask yourself, what is a problem that my book can solve? People often buy books to solve a specific problem or to gain a certain benefit. Your book has to meet the needs and the demands of the market. So doing the proper research is very important because you could publish a book in a niche or market that there's no demand for. If your trying to market and sell it but nobody really wants it then you're going to have a hard time.

Once you've identified the niche market you want to publish your book in then you need to optimize your book for specific keywords. When someone searches for that keyword, then they can find your book. Knowing the right keywords is very important. Certain keywords would be less competitive than others but if you do a better job at marketing then you can outrank a lot of the competition fairly easily. To find good keywords type your main niche keyword into the Google keyword tool to find related keywords. You can also type it slowly into the Amazon search bar and it will auto populate with relevant search terms that can more accurately define your book.

Once you have identified keywords you need to create the title. The title should be optimized and contain your main keyword. Don't make it too logical, try to have some emotion in it. The best titles offer the main benefit and intrigue people to buy the book. Think about how you're going to position your book in that niche market. If you can differentiate yourself from the other books out there that's going to be an advantage for you. There are many ways you can do that. It could be based on having more pages in your book, a more quality a book or a better cover that stands out. Or maybe it has more and information than other books. it could even be through the marketing by having more reviews than other books out there.

Now when it comes to creating the book, if it's something that you could do, then write it yourself or hire ghostwriters. Ghost writers are very common in the publishing world. A lot of books that you might see out there such as a book by Elon Musk or Donald Trump have used ghostwriters that are writing the books for them.

For ghostwriting services you can use websites such as. www.ewritersolutions.com or www.epicwrite.com

Next step is the cover and this has to stand out when people see it. It is very important in terms of getting people's attention. Try contrasting colors to what your competitors use. Also, use high quality images and designs. You can outsource designing the cover inexpensively on www.fiverr.com, for five or ten dollars. It's a good idea to order from a few different sellers just so that you can get some variety and then pick the one that you like the most, or you can even test them. That's the great thing about an e-book like this, is that you can actually test different covers. You could publish one book that has one cover for a week or two and see how it sells and then you can republish it with a different cover and see if that makes a difference.

Once you have all these materials, your ready to publish your book. Sign up for a Kindle direct publishing account (KDP). This is the platform that you can use. It's free to sign up for it and you just create a new e-book then enter in the details like the title, the description, keywords and the cover. The description should utilize good sales copy to convert the most customers. Make sure you have a good understanding of copywriting to help you with this. Then you make sure the book is formatted properly and upload it. Finally you set the price that you want to sell it at. Amazon typically will pay you a royalty from each sale for up to seventy percent. The money gets direct deposited into your bank account and they pay out every every thirty days.

The great thing about this type of business is that it's all relatively quick, once you hit the publish button your book will be live on Amazon available for sale within twenty four to forty eight hours. You can also make it available as a paperback. This is an on demand service, so you don't need any stock. When a customer orders your paperback, Amazon prints it. In KDP the option to publish a paperback version is linked in with the ebook. You just need to format your book and cover file to suit the requirements. There are some gigs on Fiverr that can help you with this.

When your book is live you must promote it and market it. This is what a lot of people neglect to do. They think that Amazon is just going to do everything for them. Marketing is what you really have to learn because long term this is what's going to allow you to really be able to make a significant amount of money online. There are a lot of books out there that are great books. But nobody knows about them because a lot of authors unfortunately are really bad marketers. The more sales you have, the better your books will rank on Amazon.

The most effective strategy is using PPC which is pay-per-click advertising on Amazon. This allows you to use sponsored adverts so you can actually pay to have your book show up next to similar books or in relevant searches. When someone clicks on the advert Amazon charges you. Facebook is also powerful when it comes to marketing outside of Amazon. With Facebook there are many strategies. There's having a fan page in the niche that you're in, it could also be a Facebook group or it could even be Facebook adverts. Build up your Facebook fan page, learn how Facebook works and start creating content for it. You can also publish adverts and promotions on Instagram, Twitter, YouTube and your blogs. Essentially you're building a brand that's going to attract people to you that you can then funnel to your book. You should also build an email list and build that relationship with them even further. Aim to diversify your streams of traffic because Amazon often change their algorithm for ranking.

Finally, you can use KDP tools such as KDP Select to make your book available for free for five days. This will encourage lots of downloads and in turn more reviews. KDP Select has a ninety day sign up period. I suggest you do it once and then take your books off it so that they are non exclusive. You can then upload them to www.draft2digital.com which will publish it in a lot of other stores. Just leave it and let it generate passive income.

How are you enjoying this book?

If you like it please share your thoughts and give it a review, thank you and enjoy the rest of the information.

Increasing Your Income With ACX

Audible/ACX is website that allows you to publish and buy an audio version of a book. Right now, the audio book business is booming and there is not much competition with only five percent of books available in audio version. If you currently have books published on Amazon, or are planning to then it is an easy and affordable way to turn your books into audiobooks and in turn increase your earnings.

The first step you need to take is publish your e-book on Amazon KDP (check the section on Kindle for more details). Once you have published it and it is live in the Amazon store head over to www.acx.com.

To add your title for sale proceed as follows. Inside there are four tabs. Go to add new title, you can search for your book here. Now you need to find a narrator, or if you have a decent voice and recording gear then you can do it yourself. Select one of the following options as suited to you.

I'm looking for someone to narrate my book
Or
I have audio files ready

Then click agree and continue. ACX will then pull your description from Amazon. You then need to add in your name, publishing year and categories. When selecting criteria for a narrator you can choose from male or female, language and voice style. Fill it in and then you just upload a couple of pages for them to use in auditions. Then click save and continue. Simple stuff.

Next is the distribution page. ACX will sell your book on Amazon, Audible and iTunes if you choose an exclusive deal. They are the best out there and it will give you better royalties to be exclusive with them so select that option. Then select how many words are in your book and Audible will calculate the estimated length. They estimate one hour to be roughly 9300 words. Always go for longer books when you write because ACX prices longer books higher, which is more money for you. The pricing scheme is as follows.

- Under 1 hour: under $7
- 1 - 3 hours: $7 - $10
- 3 - 5 hours: $10 - $20
- 5 - 10 hours: $15 - $25
- 10 - 20 hours: $20 - $30
- Over 20 hours: $25 - 35

Next you have the payment options. These are a 50/50 royalty split, or pay narrator. I suggest you pay the narrator up front. Narration is affordable, you can get a decent one for an offer of around twenty five usd per hour. Otherwise you are losing fifty percent on each sale. However if cash is tight or your not confident in your book selling then do a royalty share.

Finally you can choose how long for first the fifteen minutes to be available for review and also for how long to complete the book. Confirm everything then click to post to ACX. Narrators will then send their auditions to you for review. Listen to each one then make an offer. When they accept send them the manuscript.

When it's all done you will need to send payment and upload cover art. You should avoid stretching out your Kindle cover to

fit because it looks low quality. Create new cover art that looks similar to the Kindle cover. You will also need to have great sales copy and keywords. These can be taken from your research.

Right now ACX do not offer any advertising services but it's a good idea to contact them for promo codes for your books. They will give you fifty. You can send these to your network and ask them to review your audiobooks. Better reviews will help you get ranked higher. Again focus on creating great quality content that adds value. Finally make sure you keep scaling your books. The more you have the more your income will grow.

How to Start Affiliate Marketing

Affiliate marketing in essence is receiving a commission on sales through referrals. For example you can recommend products like headphones that you already use every single day and a earn commission off of them. The great thing about it is that you don't need any products and you don't need to worry about shipping them out. The company takes care of all of that for you so it's less hassle, less headaches and no customer service. You just get a check at the end of the day.

It's really not that hard to get started. The best program to start out with is Amazon Associates which is the number one affiliate program in the world. First off you sign up and choose any product that Amazon sells. You can basically promote it with your links. Mostly affiliates put these links on their website or they put them in the description of their YouTube videos. If you have ever watched a tech review you will often see an Amazon link in the description. That I guarantee you is an Amazon Associates link and they are earning commission off of each product.

Now, how much commission can you earn? It depends on the product category.
So for example, you can earn a six percent commission for selling headphones. So six percent of a $350 set of headphones is $21. Honestly that's pretty good considering that you don't have to buy the product or ship it out and hold inventory. Basically, Amazon takes care of everything for you.

The most popular method of affiliate marketing with Amazon is to review products and then promote them via Amazon

Associates. If you join Amazon Associates there are different rates for everything on sale. For example a vacuum can get you eight percent of every $35 sale. So you get $2.80 for every single vacuum you sell. Look around your house, look for stuff that is sold on Amazon. It doesn't have to be high ticket expensive stuff. However I do recommend that you promote high ticket items because obviously the bigger the cost of something then the more commission you get. But that doesn't mean you should neglect cheaper items which can easily sell.

You can look up any product that Amazon sells. Then all you have to do is get the link, just hit that. Boom, copy and paste this into your YouTube description or your website and from there, that's when you can start earning commission with Amazon Associates. When somebody clicks the link what happens is they get a cookie attached to their IP that lasts twenty four hours. Now here's the cool part, with Amazon if they buy anything within that twenty four hour period you actually get commission on every single thing that's in their cart. So it doesn't even have to be the product in your link.

So how do we take things a step further? This requires doing a little more work by creating an actual brand. Brands are important, and the best kind of brand is a personal brand. You can create a personal brand using YouTube which is a free platform. It doesn't cost you anything to make videos and upload them, it's all free. In addition create a website with blog posts and articles. What you can do is create a video on YouTube and also do an article on your website. It really isn't that hard to create a website blog. You can use WordPress, which is actually a free platform with some great themes. Then all you need is a domain and some web-hosting. Alternatively you can have someone build all that for you for a very reasonable price.

When you build that personal brand you can create something very powerful. We all have a story and a personality that we can share with the world. The plus side of this is that you get to build trust and a personal connection with your customers. If you were to just do the first method and you just review these things. You may get lucky and your video gets tens of thousands of views which can very well happen if you're reviewing something very popular. But where the real money starts to come in is when you become an authority figure. When people trust you, you have influence and people listen to what you have to say. So if you were to become an authority and you said that these are the best headphones of 2018 that I have tested then you guys are more likely to buy this, right?

Create consumer focused content. So what does this mean? I wouldn't be like, oh here's a link to my headphones. I would actually be like, hey guys, check it out. So I've owned twelve pairs of headphones within the last two years and these are by far my favorite Bluetooth headphones. They have perfect usability, the sound quality is amazing. Really tight sub bass and the Bluetooth and the battery life are excellent. You know what I mean? I would actually create a review, because a review gets people when they're in that phase of okay, I'm gonna go purchase a pair of headphones rather than if you're just watching a vlog of mine and I'm just like oh yeah, those are my headphones. You're not really likely to buy a $350 pair of headphones, right? So you want to create consumer focused content that really dials in when consumers are at that purchase decision when they're researching different products, they're comparing them, they're looking at reviews, that's where you want to capture your customer for the best chance of a sale.

Now the thing is, building a personal brand is not as hard as it seems. You can get started today, you don't have to be an expert. You just have to be passionate. You just have to be a person who's willing to give some valuable information to the next guy. You don't really have to do some crazy cinematics or anything like that. Once you get to a certain point of authority you can start to implement affiliate marketing by including affiliate links from Amazon Associates. Implement affiliate marketing into your personal brand and become an authority in your niche market. You should be aiming to become an authority figure in a market or niche. If you do that then you can create a very profitable website from something that you're passionate about. Now again, you don't have to really be an expert you just have to know enough to provide value to people. So for example, Beats, you don't have to be an audio expert to be able to recommend them to people who love hip hop. People who love bass, and who like that in your face sound quality, you know what I mean?

Share your hobbies and passions with the world. Once you got to a certain level, companies will started to send you their products for free in order to test out, So that's the other plus side of affiliate marketing and creating a brand is that when you build an asset like this companies come to you and they start giving you free stuff. So it's honestly a win-win, you start to earn passive income and you get freebies, I mean what's not to love? honestly creating that niche authority website, that brand really takes things to the next level. Really, if you want to succeed in this business you have to be thinking about the future.

Online courses are also a really good niche to become an affiliate for because the commissions are so high. Most of the commissions for online courses range from $100, $150, up to literally thousands of dollars for some of the really high end courses that cost $4000 and up. The good news is you don't have to be the expert because if you're someone who is a student then you can give just as much of a valid opinion as the next person. You bought the course, and you can give your actual valid opinion on it. Based on how you come across and what you say in that video you can sell a $1000 course and make a $400 commission. Basically, that's an easy way to make hundreds of dollars. If you're part of any courses right now. Honestly, just do a review on it. It doesn't even have to be all rainbows and butterflies. You can just be completely honest, throw it out there, who knows you might get a sale or two or three and boom, before you know it that's like $1000 right there.

You can also check out Clickbank Affiliate. This is similar to Amazon Affiliate, however they offer higher commissions of up to seventy five percent. In addition to focusing on physical products they also feature digital ones such as courses and tutorials. The profit per sale is very rewarding and you can earn significantly just through a few sales that click your affiliate link.

How To Make a Living On Fiverr

Fiverr is a market place where people sell their services or products from $5 upwards. There are strategies to increase the value and the amount that you can earn per sale by providing different upsells and additional add-ons as well.

To make money on Fiverr you can sell your own service or products. You might be good at something such as video editing, photo editing, graphic design, writing or any skill or service that is in demand. To give you more ideas, take a look through the categories on Fiverr.

There are a few factors that are crucial if you want to start making money on Fiverr. The first is the thumbnail of your gig. When you search for anything the thumbnail is the thing that stands out in the results. The more eye-catching and attractive the thumbnail is the more chances that someone is going to click on it and buy your gig. Test different thumbnails and see which one works best. Search in your category and look on the best-selling gigs and try to do something similar yet different.

The second most important factor is the description. You can go through your competition and have a look what kind of description they have. Analyze what works for them and do it in a similar way. Try to make it a little bit more personal, throw in a couple of jokes or something to stand out and not be as dry as your competitors. Videos can also really help convert your audience. Just explain what you do in the gig and make it more personable. You can make multiple gigs and try different descriptions and thumbnails for each to find the one that works the best.

Getting reviews is another the important factor that will define your success. Reputation on Fiverr is everything so if you see that the client is for example about to give you a bad review I recommend you to cancel the gig and this way you will save your reputation. You want to be aiming for five stars, one hundred percent, top reputation on Fiverr. This way people will have more trust in you and your gig will convert even better. Once you start getting the reviews and feedback, that's really going to boost you on Fiverr and help have your gig as a really popular premium gig. Fiverr will help promote your gigs if you have a really good service.

When you are all set, you can automate the entire Fiverr process and have a virtual assistant basically operate everything. That's the best position to be in, because then you're earning passive income. You're not going after active income where it always requires trading your time for money. With any business you still have to keep your eyes on it. You still have to oversee things, you still have to make sure things are converting and optimized.

Now how do you automate this process? Because doing a lot of these things requires a lot of time you might be wondering, how are these people on Fiverr doing this stuff for only $5? How are they really making money? When somebody would order the gig, have your virtual assistant send them an automated message with instructions on how they could get what they paid for in the gig. You can have your virtual assistant do that for you for as low as $3 an hour.

That's one way that you can automate it, and again, be able to earn profit to build a list or generate leads from. This could be sending them to another website to download information or see a video, for example. You can also upsell them on more things here such as a full course if you are just selling excerpts from it.

The key thing to success on Fiverr is to always provide more value than what people pay for. When you provide way more value they're going to become a raving fan, they're going to buy your other gigs, they're going to buy more from you and follow you on Fiverr and buy some additional things that you have as well.

How are you enjoying this book?
If you like it please share your thoughts and give it a review, thank you and enjoy the rest of the information.

How To Sell On Amazon FBA

Fulfillment by Amazon (FBA) is completely dominating the e-commerce industry. They are expanding every single day into new countries and territories. They are the absolute leader when it comes to e-commerce, which is a ridiculously high-growth industry. With Amazon FBA, they handle all of the hard work for you. You don't have to ship anything, you don't have to package anything, you don't have to create your own website and you don't have to accept payments. All of this is done by Amazon for you. So if you sell one unit a day or if you sell a thousand units a day there's no additional work on your behalf. Amazon's massive fulfillment warehouses handle this all for you and of course they take a fee for doing that, but it is well worth it.

Amazon have millions of customers and what that means for you being an Amazon seller is that you get a lot of free traffic coming to you. As long as you optimize your listing correctly and if you launch your product correctly it will show high up in the search results completely for free. You don't have to pay for that traffic which is one of the major benefits when it comes to actually selling on Amazon versus other types of e-commerce. There are five steps to being successful with Amazon FDA

Step One

Product research is the first step to finding the perfect product that is going to make you money. This is the absolute most vital step of the entire process. You can do everything else in the entire process poorly and you can still make a bunch of money. That is how good of a business model Amazon FBA is. But if you choose the wrong product, it becomes incredibly difficult to be successful on Amazon, no matter how good you are at creating a listing and marketing.

Amazon used to be a complete nightmare, looking through millions of different products literally could have taken weeks or months to do but there has been software services that have been released that take out all of the difficulty for you. The Viral Launch Tool allows you with a simple click of a button to apply a few filters and see exactly the products that you want to see with the criteria that you want. They have two pieces of software that are absolutely necessary when it comes to actually finding profitable products to sell on Amazon. The first piece of software is their web app. This goes through millions and millions of products on Amazon and you can apply different filters to actually see a specific product. So for example if you only want to see products in the baby section that have less than fifty reviews and sell on average more than $7,000 in revenue a month. Then you can literally put that into the filters and it will show you results that match. It will also give you ideas because there's such unbelievably random things that people sell on Amazon that are making thousands of dollars per month.

Essentially what you're looking for when doing product research is for products that have extremely low competition with a high amount of interest. It's the same thing as basic economics, a low amount of supply with a high level of demand. The main thing that we're looking for is products that have low reviews. Look for all the products on the page to have an average of less than fifty to seventy five reviews.

Another thing to look for is to make sure that everyone on page one has consistent revenue. If only one seller on page one of the search results has you know ten thousand dollars in revenue per month and everyone else has zero. Then maybe there's just not enough people actually searching for this particular product. For it to make sense you want to see consistent revenue and you want to see consistently low reviews. I recommend people going for products that have a monthly revenue of between seven and fifteen thousand dollars. Profit is usually about fifty percent of that but it starts to add up very quickly when you add new and profitable products to your product portfolio.

Next when doing product research you want to make sure of, is that the products that your thinking about selling are priced higher than thirteen dollars. The reason for that is that Amazon has fees for handling all of the hard work for you. If a product costs less than thirteen dollars what I've found is that Amazon's fees become too expensive. It takes up too much of your margin and thirteen dollars is about the lowest price that you can sell at as a new seller to actually be profitable. The highest price that I like look for is generally about fifty dollars. The reasoning behind this price range of thirteen to fifty dollars is people that don't recognize a brand are much less likely to make an impulse purchase if the product itself cost more than fifty dollars. The thirteen to fifty dollar range is generally the sweet spot. Remember Amazon is incredibly good at making you purchase things you didn't know that you actually needed to purchase. The entire website is designed to make you buy more things than you originally came to purchase. Therefore having a product that people are willing to buy on impulse is going to give you sales.

Last but not least, make sure that a product is not seasonal. For example Christmas stockings. These would have zero sales for eleven months a year and then have a massive spike. Look for a product with consistent demand throughout the entire year. The best tool to actually be able to see that is called Google Trends. This tool is completely free and it will tell you the average search volume and kind of popularity of any product or search term in the world over the entire year.

In summary, look for products on average that have less than fifty reviews, are priced between thirteen and fifty dollars, and are between seven and fifteen thousand dollars monthly revenue with consistent demand throughout the year. Some other things to keep in mind. Choose products that are non-breakable, small and light. so that they're not breaking in transit and not particularly complex if you have complex items people are much more likely to return them because they're not figuring out how to actually use it.

Step Two

Is finding the best supplier and actually getting that supplier to ship your product over to the USA so you can start selling them on Amazon. We're going to use a website called www.alibaba.com. Alibaba is a massive directory of all the manufacturers in China. They can literally make anything you could possibly imagine. Most of the things in your house and that anyone's wearing pretty much in the USA comes from China. Alibaba makes finding the manufacturer that you are looking for very easy. I recommend you to search by supplier. This means that you're not going to see a bunch of the same exact listings because one supplier might have a hundred product listings for the same product and if you search by product you're going to be reaching out and sending a hundred different emails to the same exact supplier. Looking by supplier will save you a bunch of time and your actually reaching out to multiple different suppliers which is very advantageous because you want to get at least three independent quotes on the product pricing.

When looking for supplier make sure to check a few things put. That they've been in business for a number of years. That they have a transaction history. That they have an online presence, a normal looking website and a phone number. To be on the safe side you can call the phone number just to make sure that they're a legitimate business. Some other things that you want to evaluate when you're talking to your supplier is how is their English, how fast are they responding and how good are they being with negotiation? You want to judge these things from the start because no two manufacturers are made equal and you want to choose the manufacturer that in the end is going to be the best long-term relationship for you both.

Once you've done some background research on your suppliers what you're going to do next is find the best three looking suppliers and you are going to ask them for a quote. One of them might give you a high price and the other a lower price. What you can then do is send the lowest quote to the others and say, hey I got this quote could you guys beat it? Oftentimes they'll come back with a better offer. Always try to negotiate the price down, which means directly more profit to your business.

Generally it takes between two and six weeks to actually get your product manufactured. So you want to factor that in when it comes to planning out when your products are actually going to arrive at Amazon. The first time you get your products manufactured generally takes a bit longer because you have to give them your logo, get your packaging design right and get the product up to spec. In addition you will get a sample sent to you which can take time as well.

The standard way that you pay a supplier is you deposit thirty percent for the entire order. Then only after they're finished and after your products have been inspected you send the last seventy percent. Inspections involve a third party or an independent party coming to the manufacturer who's making all of your products in China and say okay the products look good, the quality is there. They'll take samples and make sure everything looks completely one hundred percent ready to be shipped. Only after you actually have your product inspected do you pay that final seventy percent.

Always process payments through PayPal goods and services because you can get that money back if something goes wrong. If your supplier says they don't accept PayPal because it's more fees say okay we'll split the paypal fees 50/50. It's always worth it to do that if something goes wrong you're basically as protected as you can possibly be.

Step Three

Making a world-class, fully optimized Amazon listing. So before you can actually make a listing on Amazon you're going to have to set up your Amazon seller central account which is the platform that all sellers use to manage their inventory, to do their PPC and to create all of their listings. When you're setting up your Amazon seller central account what I recommend you do is actually choose the professional seller option. This is $39.99 per month but it allows you to sell as many units as you want every single month for no additional charge. If you choose the individual seller option you pay a one dollar fee every single time that you sell a product. So if you sell forty or less per month the individual plan probably makes sense for you. But you professional Amazon sellers people that intend to do this as a source of income are going to sell more than forty units a month.

To go about creating your product listing what you're going to do is, go to the create a new product listing section and then choose the relevant product category for your products. First of all is your product name which you need to fully optimize because it's very important from a search engine optimization perspective to have a lot of the keywords that your customers are going to eventually type into Amazon. Your title is paramount when it comes to actually ranking organically for all the search terms that your customers are going to potentially search. Next you put in your manufacturing name. This is the name that's going to actually show up as your seller store name on Amazon. Anytime you look for a product and click on a product listing in Amazon you can see the name of the sellers store right in blue over off to the right your brand name. You want to keep it fairly universal because later on you might want to expand into other things. Therefore naming your company something very specific is not a good thing in the long run. Name it something more general so you can have more products under your actual umbrella.

Next up your going to put in the product ID which is a universal product code (UPC). This is the actual numerical code that actually creates the barcode that's unique to every single product in the world. To be on the safe side I do recommend purchasing your barcodes as Amazon tends to prefer this. You need to then give your manufacturer the actual bar code that they are going to print on every single one of your products. How that generally works is you send them a PDF that has the barcode. They print off that PDF and put stickers on the outside of the box of each one of your units. What I recommend is having them actually apply it as a sticker to your product packaging. The reason for them actually printing it on the product packaging is because sometimes those printers aren't high enough quality and then later on down the line Amazon might not be able to actually scan it. Make sure that all of your boxes have made in China printed on them along with your logo and brand name, product barcode printed on a sticker and attached to each box as well product photography. If you want to be successful selling on Amazon don't be cheap when it comes to product photos

The next part is where you set your price. A lot of people make a mistake here and they'll set their price too low. Initially set your price at the highest possible amount you could ever see yourself selling your product. The reason for that is something called a price band restriction. So if you say for example you set your product price to $20, Amazon will not let you go higher but they will let you go down. So set your price at the highest you could ever realistically imagine yourself selling it and you can always lower it at any time. This will allow you to do special discounts and so on.

The last part of creating a fully optimized listing is making sure that your keywords are on point. How to research keywords? As an example let's say that your selling a garlic press. You would type in garlic into the Amazon search bar. Then you would see all of the related words to it because not everyone calls a garlic press a garlic press. Some people call it a garlic mincer some people call it you know a stainless steel garlic press or a jumbo garlic press. Overall what you're looking for here is all of the other highest volume search terms that somebody could type in wanting a garlic press. Add as many of those search terms to your bullet points, product description, title and of course to your back end keywords

Step Four

Is getting those first initial reviews and how to actually launch your product to page one. The only legitimate option when it comes to getting those first vital reviews is what is called, Amazon early reviewer program. It costs sixty US dollars and for that price Amazon incentivizes people to leave you a review. I recommend everyone to always participate in this program. For sixty dollars you get five reviews which equals about twelve dollars per review. That is a very good price to get reviews especially because it's so difficult now to actually get reviews any other way. The service is available in the advertising menu under Amazon early reviewer program. Always make sure that you have some reviews before you start your launch because think about it again logically. If you see a product on Amazon that has zero reviews are you going to buy it?

The next step is what's called the launch phase during which you have a promotion or a giveaway. First off you should generate coupon codes inside Amazon seller central. With these you would giveaway units of your product at a percentage off to people out there in the world who are couponers that want a good deal. If you sell more units per day Amazon's algorithm is going to say okay this product must be better, it's selling more let's rank it organically number one. Then more people will see it. The more units that sell, the more money Amazon makes and they want to obviously reward the people who are selling the most.

Step Five

Amazon Pay Per Click (PPC) is another powerful way to actually get additional sales and increase in your organic ranking for different keywords. There are two main options that you have available at your disposal for Amazon PPC. These are, automatic campaigns and manual campaigns. Automatic campaigns basically pull keywords from your listing and it takes all of those keywords and it automatically creates permutations of applicable keywords that it thinks people might be typing related to your listing. Automatic campaigns are extremely easy to create literally with a click of a button and Amazon does all of the hard work for you. The problem with automatic campaigns is generally they aren't as profitable because Amazon's testing a lot of things that aren't likely to work. To counter this, the strategy you can use with automatic campaigns is instead of creating one automatic campaign with fifty dollars per day, create ten automatic campaigns with five dollars per day. Then what you do is you pause all the ones that aren't performing and you scale up the daily spend of the ones that are performing.

For manual campaigns what you to do is you can look at the top performing sellers in any niche and you can find the exact words that they're ranking for and that they're using in their PPC campaigns. Then you can take those words and apply them to your own manual PPC campaigns.

Blog for a Living

What is a blog? Essentially a blog is a regularly updated page website. It is created and centered around regularly updated content and blog posts. The Huffington Post our BuzzFeed are both examples of websites that would mainly be considered a blog. Nowadays you can make a full-time income from blogging. However it's not easy and it's not an overnight success unless you're extremely lucky or you've got some really impressive connections.

Contrary to popular belief, blogs are not just an online diary about your thoughts. You can blog about whatever your heart desires, it can be company updates, a product you like, a workout you recommend to your friend or as a creative outlet to practice your writing a way to meet others and connect. There are infinite ways and infinite things that you can blog about it's really all up to you basically anything you can think.

When comes to getting traffic to your blog, the first thing to learn search engine optimization matters (SEO). SEO determines what shows up in the top of the rankings when you type in some phrase. You can pay to be in that top by using Google AdWords. Also showing to Google that you have a quality website through optimization and quality content will help you reach the top of the rankings.

To monetize your blog you can use Google AdSense. How this works is that you sign up for a free Google AdSense account, and then you get Google's code, you copy that, paste that into your website. Google will match which companies are willing to advertise for different search terms that are found on your site. It's by far one of the easiest ways that you can monetize your site. All you have to do is write the content, copy and paste the code from Google AdSense, onto your site and then your done. To become more successful you need to have a high rank for these relevant search terms.

As you write more high quality content your traffic will increase. You want to be the first person to write about new things in your niche. Networking with other bloggers will give you a clear view of what's going to happen in the future. Ask yourself what is potentially going to change in my category that no one else has wrote about yet? You can be the second or third person but if you publish a good piece of content that's better than anything else out there, then you can potentially outrank them, and also get more social shares out of it.

Another income stream you can add to your blogging is to incorporate affiliates. With affiliate marketing you're representing a company that offers a product or service that you believe in, preferably one that you've tried out yourself. If you write about them and mention them on your blog and if one of your readers clicks that link, and then opens an account with that affiliate or buys a product through that link from that affiliate then you get paid a small commission. Make sure you're representing affiliates that you believe in, that you trust. If you're just signing up to be an affiliate for some company just to earn a quick buck, your readers are going to know.

How are you enjoying this book?
If you like it please share your thoughts and give it a review, thank you and enjoy the rest of the information.

Udemy Course Creation

If you're somebody who is thinking about teaching online or wants to get involved with it then creating your own online courses with Udemy is a great way to start. If you put in enough time, energy and effort you can definitely gain great financial results. It can eventually become a passive income stream where you can probably spend less than fifteen minutes a week on it. Udemy does a lot to promote your courses and they currently have over twelve million students on their platform so it's kind of a built-in audience.

When starting out the first step is the production of the course. For beginners you can use some basic video and microphone equipment. Smartphones are pretty good for video these days, but make sure you get a decent microphone for the audio. You can tape up a piece of paper as a makeshift teleprompter underneath the camera. Plan out your course with some slides or live footage, depending on your subject. Try to mix it up with screen sharing segments or PowerPoint segments where you are walking through an actual process. Add in screen share shots like talking head stuff and even written parts, quizzes and so on. Mix up the content so that its not just you lecturing in from the camera for five hours because that would probably generate some negative feedback. Try to make your segments around two to ten minutes long. Keeping lectures short makes it feel like it's building momentum for the students going through your course.

With marketing it's really similar to Amazon in that you know when you're launching a book you have to give it that initial marketing push and then let the algorithm try and take notice.

Try to generate a critical mass of enrollments of students and reviews because both of those metrics are pretty prominent on the sales page. You can create free coupons to send out to your peers, colleagues and other authors. Say, hey check this out here's a free coupon and if you like it, drop in a review. Also share the coupons in Facebook coupon groups and on coupon sites. At the start you can also set the course price for free. Aim for about one thousand enrollments and then set your price. Interact with your students, send them welcome notices and keep them engaged with course updates. If your content it good then they are more likely to buy your other courses. You should always be creating more courses and improving along the way.

Finally, if you have a podcast, YouTube channel or online presence you can share your course there.

Build & Optimize A Professional Shopify

Creating a drop shipping company is one of the best business models for beginners using Shopify. If you've ever bought something from Ebay there's a chance that you bought it from someone drop shipping. You don't have to invest money up front and Shopify does all the hard design work for you.

First off sign up with Shopify and choose a store name. The store name will appear in the free domain that Shopify is going to give you. Next you are going to choose a product on a website called Aliexpress. This is a Chinese website where suppliers sell directly. You can find many cheap products that are still good quality. You are going to list the same product with the same images and description on your ecommerce store that you are going to create with Shopify. Obviously you will list it on your store for a higher price. Whenever you receive an order you confirm the payment and the customers address. Then you go to Aliexpress, order the product and ship it directly to the customer and you keep the difference.

You can do it wherever you are in the world as long as you have an internet connection and a computer. Aliexpress ships to the United States without you having to touch any of the items. You don't have to do anything, just press a button. You might be thinking, can the customer go directly on Aliexpress and order that product by themselves? Yes they can but in ninety nine percent of the cases people want simplicity because most people don't even know Aliexpress exists and also people buy from where it's most familiar and convenient.

When it comes to selecting a product there are some fundamental things you need to be aware of. If you get this right then you are going to be successful with Shopify. Whatever niche you choose, make sure it is a passionate niche. In fact there's a big difference between what people need and what people are passionate about. When people need something they go on Amazon and buy from there. They don't even think about your Shopify store. However if you sell something unique and interesting that people are passionate about then you are going to have success. Here are some examples of niches that people have passion for. People really love their pets, obviously there is a dog niche divided into many different sub niches. People that own a Labrador, a golden retriever or whatever dog breed. You can find t-shirts and accessories for those specific people. The golf niche is very passionate and people usually have plenty of money. Camping and survival people really love these activities and buy these gear and accessories. Gardening, cycling, hiking, fishing, all these activities and sports people, they love doing them. Be a little bit creative and find products that these people might enjoy and want to buy. The best way to do this is to actually combine these niches. For example if you want to get into the cat niche then you want to find accessories and jewelry related to cats. In this way you're targeting a specific audience who loves cats but they also love jewelry, bracelets, necklaces or whatever.

For more ideas use Aliexpress and check the categories section. You will find that there are many categories and many, many subcategories. For example, jewelry, necklaces and pendants, rings, trendy earrings, bracelets, bangles etc. Once you find a product you can import all the details to your Shopify store.

There are two things that you have to check for when choosing a product on Aliexpress. The first one is the shipping, look for quick and cheap. Most suppliers offer free shipping, but one to two dollars is fine. When shipping to The United States it's usually quite fast, between twelve to twenty days. For The United Kingdom you'll see that it's usually at least twenty to forty days. Avoid all the shippings that are over twenty days. The customers will be upset, therefore sending to The United States is always the easiest and cheapest option.

The second thing you have check is the seller rating. To do this in the search page, move your mouse over a product and see the icons that appear. We always want to find products that have at least three diamonds and less than four crowns. In this range sellers are established and reliable but still not too premium and so the prices are still reasonable. Products with five crowns are a little bit more expensive. Always avoid the medals because these are new sellers or maybe they have bad reviews so stay away from them. Price wise I recommend products from zero to ten dollars on Aliexpress so that you can resell them from five to thirty dollars on your Shopify store.

When you have chosen a product you will need to then design and customise your Shopify store. First of all install a theme. The theme is basically controlling how your website looks. You can then customize this to display your products, text and images as you prefer. Add a countdown timer because scarcity is a very powerful sales method. When a product is available for a limited time customers are more likely to buy immediately. You can explore the app store and find hundreds of apps for your Shopify store. In the beginning you want to keep it simple and start with a few apps and then when you are making money there is no problem in buying more apps.

Traffic is the lifeblood of your business. You can have the most beautiful store in the world but if you don't send traffic to it, then you won't make any money. There are two ways to send traffic to your website. The first one is to pay for the traffic and the second one is to use free traffic methods. When you use paid traffic you have complete control over it and also it's reliable and predictable. While if you don't have any money there are free traffic methods but you have less control over them. Most people get scared of using paid traffic because they think they have to invest thousands of dollars. It's crazy how people are not willing to invest a few bucks in something that could potentially make them thousands of dollars. There are so many traffic sources where you can buy traffic. The most popular is Facebook and with over two billion users the potential is huge. You don't need a huge budget, you can start with three or more dollars a day. Create and install the Facebook pixel in your Shopify store to enable this.

Instagram influencers can also help promote your store. Try to find people with a big following in your niche. Instead of paying them up front you can offer to share revenue so that you don't have to invest anything. You can also use paid Google adverts to rank for keywords relevant to your niche. When someone searches for your products your store should be near the top of the first page of results.

Ghost Production: Make Money from Your Music

If your a music producer with some hot beats you can easily make money online with ghost producing. Ghost producing essentially is making songs and then selling them to other people. There are different levels, at one extreme you're making songs for people and just selling the songs to them that they can then repackage up and market as their own. Then at the other extreme you're basically helping someone on a track without getting explicit credit in the track title. You may even get credit in the official release notes or as a featured artist on the actual track.

To get started make lots and lots of commercially viable songs. If you're working in an obscure genre that doesn't have a lot of money flowing into it then there will be less successful and rich people who would be interested to buy your music. If you want to make decent money then you need to follow the money.

You can sell your music at sites such as the following:

https://www.edmghostproducer.com
Connecting up and coming DJs with Ghost Producers, EDM Ghost Producer is the perfect intermediate for both buying and selling custom made tracks online.

https://www.ghostproducing.com
Produce original or remix according to your ideas. Do you need help about finishing your music? We can finish it for you and turn it to a quality class music!

https://houseoftracks.com/
Build a career from music production. Sell your tracks to a huge customer base.

Upwork and Fiverr are also great websites where you can offer your music and music production services.

A further step you can take is to proactively reach out to people who might be in the position to purchase a song. At the one extreme you might have a sort of popular DJ and at the other extreme you have something more interesting a celebrity. Have you seen how many sort of TV actors and sort of personalities in the world also do DJing? Now most of these celebrity DJ's don't actually release music currently but they should do and that's where you come in as the ghost producer. What you can do is approach the manager of this celebrity. This is where you need a lots of tracks because if you just come to them with one track and you say this is my track, do you want to buy it? Then they're going to say no probably because music is subjective.

So what you need to do is approach them with at least five different tracks and then hopefully they'd like a few or just even one of your tracks. Then ideally what will happen are a few things. One option is they just like it as it is and they will just buy it or offer you some sort of like royalty for work. If they offer you royalties then that's great because you will get a consistent revenue from any sales. Another option is maybe they like most of it but wants a little bit of a tweak and that's absolutely cool.

The potential money that can be earned from ghost producing is huge. Some hip hop ghost producers are known for charging fees of fifteen thousand dollars and up for a song. For beginners five hundred dollars is a good start.

YouTube: Monetize & Attract More Viewers

Youtube is a great way to earn money online. If your someone who has a lot of followers online then there's a few different ways to bring in revenue. One is through monetizing your videos and getting paid through Advertising with Google Adsense. Recently YouTube has changed the rules to join the program. In the past adverts were showing up on videos that weren't really advertiser friendly. Nowadays you need a minimum of four thousand hours of watch time and a minimum of one thousand subscribers.

To be successful with Adsense on YouTube the key strategy would be to get a lot of views. The advertising revenue is basically going off that the more views you get the more money you make. Therefore if you want to earn a decent income then you must make content that will bring in lots of views. Every time someone watches one of your videos, adverts will appear either on the sides of the videos, before it starts or sometimes in the middle of a video. These adverts are what will earn you money, and sometimes people don't even need to click on them for you to still make a profit from them.The typical pay rate is two dollars for every thousand views. So if your goal is to earn a thousand dollars extra, you would need a half a million views to get a thousand dollars. But don't worry, the good news is there's tons of people crushing it that have small views but they're monetizing in other ways. One thing you can do with YouTube adverts is if you really niche your channel down and go into certain niches that have higher click through, you can start earning some decent money.

The second way to earn money with YouTube is affiliate marketing. You can start getting custom links from Amazon Associates or other affiliate programs and paste them into your YouTube video description and then you can make money when someone clicks the link (see Affiliate Marketing chapter for more information). The next way to monetize your YouTube Channel is through brand deals, whether that means a sponsored video or a shout-out in a video. When working with a brand, never work with a product you do not believe in or message you don't agree with. Once you start trying to sell you it can sometimes end up devaluing your content and in turn devaluing that brand.

Remember, YouTube will often go through multiple phases and algorithm changes that affects a lot of smaller creators revenue. Keep up to date with the changes and adapt as required.

Make Money With Envato

Envato is the world's largest digital assets provider. Everything is available here including, web templates, code, photos, videos, music, presets and much more. You could for example sell your codes for some apps or some software anything or maybe some video graphics or Photoshop templates. There are so many options, for ideas head over to Envato and see what is selling now.

As a case study, you might design a website template and sell it on Envato for fifty dollars, a thousand times in a year and make some real money. The reality is this you have the ability to sell it as many times as possible throughout the entire lifetime of that piece of intellectual property. It's a practical time investment to make a product or something that can be resold multiple times. Therefore make the extra effort to make products that you can resell. You can even buy intellectual rights for some products and sell them. It could also maybe a variation of that. Essentially your selling that and making some great passive income.

You might want to check out Envato if you're a creative person and skilled with different softwares, making music, or videos. For example, you can create templates for wordpress sites through Envato's themeforest, and every time someone decides to go with your creations you will get paid. If you're skilled with creating music, upload some sick tunes and you will create a passive income stream if people buy your tunes. If you have great photography skills or design skills, share them there.

Envato also offer an affiliate program. You can sign up for this and when your done find any Envato products, then just paste your link and share where you want to promote.

How are you enjoying this book?
If you like it please share your thoughts and give it a review, thank you and enjoy the rest of the information.

Setup A Successful Patreon

Patreon is a membership platform that makes it really easy for creators to get paid. It is a crowdsourcing type of income model that's based entirely around rewards and incentives that you the content creator get to design for your own audience. The concept comes from the idea of patronage which is actually a really old idea. Mozart, Shakespeare and Da Vinci they all had patrons, mostly aristocrats who paid them to create so they could enjoy their works and brag to their friends about how cool they are for supporting creators. In essence it's kind of like that but better because this provides creators with a sustainable income while retaining creative control and it allows fans to connect with them on a whole new level. So if you're a professional creator start a page and give your fans the opportunity to become patrons. Different people are trying to find a way to monetize their creative content and keep pursuing the things that they're passionate about. Patreon offers a great to do that and it could help you create the best work of your life.

Assuming you have a following and people are fans of what you do, you can set up a Patreon account and let your fans subscribe to you. They can then decide on how much they want to donate to you. When you sign up you'll be greeted by a display name. I highly recommend using something that you use on your page, or your book, or your album or wherever you're producing content. Whatever name you go by there have it be the same name here on Patreon. It's just going to make it much easier to find you. You're also going to have a profile picture. This is the same type of profile picture that you have on your YouTube channel or wherever else you are. You really want your cover image to reflect your personality and what you do in the best possible way. Maybe that's just having a thing that says your brand with the times you stream or the times you release videos, or something else entirely. Be creative.

Next you're going to have some social media links. Include all of the social media, the more the better. Facebook, YouTube, Instagram, Twitter all that stuff, include it. Next, move to your About section. This is huge, think of this as your sales pitch. It is the only opportunity you have to convince someone to invest their hard-earned money in you and your creative products. This should be a short little paragraph about what people can expect from you but way more important than just this text part is your intro video. This is not an introduction of your YouTube channel or book or twitch or short stories. This is an introduction of Patreon to your existing audience on whatever platform they are on. While Patreon does have a really great search function, the majority of your new Patrons are not going to come from the website itself. Instead they'll come from the traffic that you kick up on your platform where they already know you.

Just as important as the About section is your reward tiers. This is what sets Patreon apart from YouTube or Twitch or other crowdsourcing sites. You can create as many or as few tiers as you choose and you get to create them specifically for your own audience which is different than any other audience on earth. You should use that to your advantage when creating these reward tiers. The most important thing is not to create more work for yourself. Writing a personalized thank you message for every patron might sound like a great idea but when your Patreon starts booming and you have to create a hundred individual thank you messages you aren't spending time doing the thing people are paying you to begin with.

The best reward tiers you can design are ones that happen alongside the work you are already doing. Such as creating credits at the end of a video or using people's names and short stories. Think about what you want from your favorite creator or what you would want from your favorite creator because believe it or not you are somebody's favorite. It's very important to put yourself in others shoes while designing these reward tiers. Finally don't make too many reward tiers, too many choices and people will tend to get overwhelmed. It's more important that you feel like people are getting an adequate reward then for you to have a ton of reward tiers. If you have the perfect hundred dollar tier don't be afraid to use it, honestly the reward far outweighs the amount.

Finally after setting up everything you have one last thing to do and that is to set up your goals. Start small and attainable, people will want to help you reach those goals. If you start with something crazy and unattainable or not entirely realistically, people might not want to waste their money and see you not reach that goal. People are more likely to spend the money if you are close to the goal or if they can have a significant contribution to the goal. Update these goals often and be sure to include rewards in these goals for all the patrons who helped you reach it.

Take your time before the launch of your Patreon. Make sure everything is exactly how you want it and remember never give up.

Bonus: Why People Fail Online

There are three main reasons why people fail to make money online. This all revolves around one similar theme and that is a lack of focus. You can be as lazy as you want but if you're unfocused you're not going to be successful with making money online.

Reason One

What often will happen as a beginner is you will have a tendency to jump from one method to another. So if you're here right now because you want to learn affiliate marketing, at some point you're going to get distracted and you're going to go after mobile marketing or you might consider creating a YouTube channel. There are literally hundreds of different ways to make money online, way more than in this book. Now as a beginner you have to figure out what's best for you. So during your beginning phase it's all about figuring out which of the ways to make money online is best for you. Maybe you work full time and have a few hours spare or you recently quit your job. Figure out what works best for you. You should try a few ideas but eventually you need to cut that out and stick with one thing that you like, that works for you. When you stick with one it is your job is to master that one.

Reason Two

People tend to give up right before they find the diamond. There is a famous story about a guy who started a mining company. He bought all this equipment, got loans from friends and family and then he started digging a hole in this spot that he thought had gold in it. About ten feet down he found some gold so he started pressing on farther and farther. He went down to almost three hundred feet, without finding any more gold so he gave up and he folded the company. Three years later someone else went back to that exact same hole and dug three feet down farther than the guy did before and that's when they found one of the biggest gold mines in the history of that particular state. On the internet this story is very common, people get so far and reach that breaking point. Then because of emotions and lack of faith in their method they give up right before they start making a lot of money. This happens all the time, so if that's you, make sure you continue to push through. Check out other stories of people working in the same field for inspiration. You will be surprised and you can relate with their struggles.

Reason Three

You find a winning income stream and for whatever reason decide it will be best to let that go and keep it earning steady while you try and find something else. Maybe it's another niche, or another method. So what will happen is this first thing keeps making money but eventually because your focus is now elsewhere the income starts to drop and eventually goes away. What you should do is, once you find that one winning thing it doesn't matter if it's a one affiliate site or a YouTube channel. Once you find that one winner you have to hammer away at that winner until there's nothing left for you to gain anymore. Alright, so that means you keep creating content, you keep creating videos, try to get some paid at traffic in there, try to create your own products. Once you get that winner hammer that thing out until there is nothing left for you to gain from it.

Ok, so keep that in mind those are the three main reasons people fail.

Stay focused, persistent and think positive about your future.

I wish you all the best.

Bonus: Inspirational Stories

Kelly, 26 Years Old. Former Truck Driver

I've had two main jobs and in my life which were pretty grueling. I didn't have a whole lot of hope for my future. I had dropped out of college a couple times because I'm one of those personality types. I have a hard time making myself do something that I really don't like. I didn't have a lot of interest in college so I just could not make myself go with it. Then I chained myself nine to five employment. My first job was a call center worker. If any of you that have a call center background of tech support or customer service support then you know that can be pretty grueling. After a couple years of that I became a truck driver. I was just really looking for things to get me out of the call center position. I saw the idea of becoming a team truck driver because I really needed a change in my life and you can actually make some good money as a truck driver. To briefly summarize the truck driving experience, let's just say a week or two on the road had me wanting to go back to the call center. You live in the truck, they don't really even want you to stop to stock up on food like at Walmart they want you to just stop eat at the truck stops and that's why you see so many unhealthy truckers. It's really a road to the bottom faster than you wouldn't believe.

I just couldn't take it so after four months I quit. I had a decent amount of money but was still pretty depressed feeling like my life wasn't really going anywhere. It felt like I will live in a cycle of poverty for the rest of my life if I did not make a change. So I tried to make money online. Actually I had tried that on and off since I was twenty years old but that time I was still lazy and not ready to devote myself. This time I was more serious. I got involved with some courses on how to make money online. I threw myself into the training and I followed everything that the training said to do. Everyday I took action and actually stuck with it, day in and day out. I remember making my first little bit and then being inspired and growing it.

During that time i had gone back to the call center job to make sure my income was stable. But after one year I actually quit my job when I started to make good money online. I haven't looked back, I mean basically I just kept doing what I was doing. I devoted myself to it and followed a routine.

If I didn't make that change and choose to learn how to make money online I was gonna go into my later years stuck in the cycle of poverty. I just made the decision no more no more. When you decide to turn that switch on it is what's going to completely transform your life

Steve, 34 Years Old. Former Fitness Instructor

A year and a half ago I worked at LA Fitness. I've always fought with this idea that I wanted to work for myself, be my own boss because I just hate being you know told to do stupid things by people that I don't really respect. I got really tired of that at my last job. I remember there was a time I had to work two weeks straight with no days off. I was miserable and I didn't like what I was doing. That really made me open my eyes to the reality that have to work smart because I saw guys there making $40,000 but they were putting in like a 9:00 in the morning to 10:00 at night sometimes just dealing with all sorts of crap. I got so tired of it and seeing them what I realized is I was looking at them and I was like these guys are working really hard but they're not really doing anything. The flurries of activity where you know you're doing a lot of stuff but it's not really getting you anywhere you're not being smart about what you're doing.

Moving forward on time I enrolled in a social media marketing agency program. What that is in short is you run social media for small businesses that are not very known on social media like a little restaurant or a little salon or whatever it is and you help them get traffic. They pay you per month to run that social media and I got into that. After some time I ran into this barrier where I didn't like social media marketing I was like maybe there's just something wrong with me like I'm being too whiny or I'm just I need to just get over it or whatever. I felt like this is still not right for me.

Later on I found out about selling on Amazon and I was so excited because you could make money online but you didn't have to sell you never even have to talk on the phone. I took courses to speed up my learning curve tremendously. My business grew fast as I gained more knowledge. I was inspired by the results and it just keeps growing.

Eventually I was able to quit my fitness job and now work for myself.

Thanks for Reading!

What did you think of, **Make Money Online: Twelve Proven Methods To Earn Passive Income And Work From Anywhere in the World**

I know you could have picked any number of books to read, but you picked this book and for that I am extremely grateful.

I hope that it added at value and quality to your everyday life. If so, it would be really nice if you could share this book with your friends and family by posting to Facebook and Twitter.

If you enjoyed this book and found some benefit in reading this, I'd like to hear from you and hope that you could take some time to post a review. Your feedback and support will help this author to greatly improve his writing craft for future projects and make this book even better.

I want you, the reader, to know that your review is very important and so, if you'd like to leave a review, all you have to do is click here and away you go. I wish you all the best in your future success!

Thank you and good luck!

Max Lane 2019

The Fastlane to Make Money Online: How to Write a Book and Make Passive Income with Self Publishing, Audiobooks and More

Max Lane

Copyright Notice

No part of this book may be reproduced or transmitted in any form whatsoever, electronic, or mechanical, including photocopying, recording, or by any information storage or retrieval system without expressed written, dated and signed permission from the author. All copyrights are reserved.

Disclaimer

Reasonable care has been taken to ensure that the information presented in this book is accurate. However, the reader should understand that the information provided does not constitute legal, medical or professional advice of any kind.

No Liability: this product is supplied "as is" and without warranties. All warranties, express or implied, are hereby disclaimed. Use of this product constitutes acceptance of the "No Liability" policy. If you do not agree with this policy, you are not permitted to use or distribute this product.

We shall not be liable for any losses or damages whatsoever (including, without limitation, consequential loss or damage) directly or indirectly arising from the use of this product.

Can I Ask You a Quick Favor?

If you like this book, I would greatly appreciate if you could leave an honest review

Reviews are very important to us authors, and it only takes a minute to post.

Download Audio

This book is also available now as an audiobook.
Head over to www.audible.com or
Download it on the Audible application

In This Book You Will Discover

Self publishing on Amazon and Audible is **the easiest and fastest** way to make money online right now. If you're looking for a **passive income** that can provide you with an extra $1000 to $10,000 and upwards a month, with little work involved, well then there is no greater way than this. *The best thing about it is that you only have to do the work once!*

Everything You Need to Know in One Book

Creating a self publishing business is probably easier than you think and **it is still in the early stages**. In this book, you'll gain access to revolutionary advice that is guaranteed to **make you money** around the clock. For the price of a lunch, you will discover how to make your book outrank the best sellers on Amazon, earn a fortune through low competition audiobooks and much, much more. The publishing process is fun, fulfilling and profitable. In fact you can repeat the process as many times as you want and generate even more **passive income!**

Take a moment to think about what your life would be like when you start earning a passive income

What would you be doing? How would you be spending your time? What would you do with the extra money?

Start your journey now towards making money with Self Publishing on Amazon, Kindle Publishing and Audible

Free Mentoring

Do you want to achieve **better results** for your kindle business?

Mentoring is the **proven** way

Book your **free** twenty publishing mentoring session now

maxlifealarm@gmail.com

Introduction

Find A Profitable Niche
    Researching for Audible
    The Top Five Niches
        Top Niche Number Six
        Top Niche Number Five
        Top Niche Number Four
        Top Niche Number Three
        Top Niche Number Two
        Top Niche Number One

Write a Title That Sells
    Step One: Competition
    Step Two: Customer Research
        2A. Researching Amazon
        2B. Researching Forums
        2C. Researching Youtube
        2D. Researching Successful companies,
        2E. Researching Udemy
    Step Three: The Title

Covers That Convert
    ACX Cover

How to Write Book Descriptions That Sell
    Step One: Description Headline
    Step Three: Call to Action

How to Write Your Book Super Fast
    Become The Writer
    Have Your Books Written Fast and Cheap

Specifications
Writing Services
    Epic Write
    E-Writer Solutions (EWS)
    Urban Writers
    The Writing Summit
    Upwork

How to Format Your Book
Title, Sub Title and Author Name
Disclaimer
Offer
Other Books By
Content
Book Contents
Last Page
Paperback Formatting

How To Publish Your Book on KDP
Keywords
Categories
Releasing Your Book
KDP Select
Paperback
Price Advice

ACX
Bounty Program

Marketing and Promotion
Social Media Marketing
    Twitter
    Facebook

    YouTube
    Email Marketing
    Book Promotion Sites
        Buckbooks
        Booksbutterfly
        BookBub
        Bknights

Reviews and Launching Your Book
    ACX reviews

Sell More Books With AMS Ads
    Summary
    Monitor Your Campaigns
    A/B Testing Your AMS Ad Campaigns
    Create an A/B Test
    Most Worthwhile Things To Change:
    Avoid These Common Mistakes

Make Even More Money With Bundles

Building a Brand
    Author Page

Your Book Not Selling?

Conclusion

Introduction

Amazon has changed the way people are reading books. Customers are being presented with better options and this is increasing spending. Nowadays you can easily buy books from Amazon in digital, paperback and audio formats. The market is huge and every year it has been growing. This presents a lucrative opportunity for entrepreneurs like us to be able to publish books and make money online through three distinct sources. Ebook, audiobook and paperback. This introduction will outline the basics of publishing to you. There is of course a lot more to it which will be covered in the following chapters. For now it is about simplifying the process to give you an overview of it. It is then your decision if you want to take things further.

When it comes to publishing oftentimes people think that they have this amazing idea for a book and that everybody will love it. Then when they finally put it out there, they find that it just does not sell. Oftentimes it's because they did things in the wrong way or the wrong order. The number one, most important thing when you're publishing a book on Amazon is choosing the niche or market that you're publishing the book in. First and foremost you have to research what's selling on Amazon and what it is that people are searching for.

Amazon is one of the biggest search engines in the world. People visit there with an idea, type in a keyword and then find a book that fits it for them. That's how a lot of people are buying books, unless they know a specific title of what that book is, or the author or whatever that might be. Amazon is a unique marketplace with certain topics that will sell a lot better than others and that's why initial research is always very important. As a publisher you can't try to reinvent the wheel or create a new market from scratch. It is your responsibility to identify what people are searching for, what's hot, what's selling and what's making money. Now there are distinct ways that you can research that and see how well certain books are selling as well as looking at the bigger picture of the business. Because once you get started with making money through Amazon you want to be able to grow beyond it. Realize that there is more to this then just publishing on Amazon. If you find a profitable niche it can allow you to create other streams of income and build a brand around it. Then those customers are yours. Therefore doing this preliminary market research at the start is the most important thing. You have to find the demand, what people are searching or what is a problem that your book can solve. Often times people buy books to solve a specific problem or to gain a certain benefit. Your book has to meet the needs and demands of the market. We will take a detailed look at this in later chapters.

Fundamentally the way that Amazon works is it's a search engine and so you have to optimize your book for specific keywords. When someone searches for that keyword, then they can find your book. Therefore knowing which keywords to use is very important. Once you've identified that you will need to create a title and think about how you are going to position your book in that market. If you can differentiate yourself from the other books out there in a positive way then it will be a distinct advantage for you. At the same time you need to stay relevant to your market. Differentiating your book is a very powerful marketing tactic and there's many ways you can do that. You could differentiate based on having more pages in your book, a higher quality book, a better cover that stands out more or maybe a better title that offers different benefits or solves a unique problem. It could even be through the marketing by having more reviews than the other books out there. Maybe it's offering a bonus that can go along with your book that no one else is really doing. Or maybe you're standing out because you're building a brand in that niche and building a relationship with people by marketing to them in other ways outside of Amazon. In turn you're giving more value to your potential customers than anyone else. These are all critical components that will affect your books success. You must focus on each one by one and master them effectively.

When it comes to creating the book it's something that you could write yourself or it can be done by hiring ghostwriters. First of all you need a great title and the right keywords to get you going. These can be decided on by researching your market effectively. Take a look at what your customers are saying. Take a look at your competitors. When it comes to writing the book writing it yourself is a great way to really understand your niche and even better if your on a budget. Otherwise, ghost writers are very common in the publishing world. A lot of books out there were written by ghostwriters. Donald Trump, Elon Musk, Nelson Mandela and other famous celebrities are unlikely to have time to write the books themselves. Ghostwriters can take care of the writing and research for you. They have the level of expertise that you might not be able to have and they can write a book for you that's of great quality. It's the same sort of thing if you hire a graphic designer to design a cover or images or banners for you. Or you might hire a web designer to design a website for you. You're basically paying them to create something for you which you then own the rights to.

The most important thing to consider in the writing process is quality because your book has to be something that will ideally yield a positive review. Positive reviews will influence better sales and reputation. The quality doesn't have to be perfect because the beauty of publishing is you can put it out there, get feedback on it and then you can consistently make it better. A lot of people wait to put something out there until it is perfect. But quality is something that evolves over time. For example the iPhone has constantly been made better and better throughout the years. You should do that with any book that you might publish, continually revise and improve it.

When you have your book written your going to want to design a cover. This will include your title and pen name. The cover has to stand out in a positive way when people see it. They have to think, I want to buy that. Designing a cover is something you can outsource inexpensively. Websites like Fiverr offer many great designers who are experienced in the publishing business and can create a great cover for you for just five to ten dollars. Then you can even test them out to see what works. That's a great thing about a publishing is that you can actually test out different covers. You could publish one book with one cover for a week or two and see how it sells. Then you can republish it with a different cover and see if that makes a difference to the sales.

Once you have all this wrapped up, your ready to publish your book and to do that you can set up a Kindle direct publishing account (KDP). This is the platform that allows you to publish ebooks and paperbacks on. It's free to sign up for and you put in the details like the title, the description, the keywords, the cover and so on. Then simply you upload your book which should be formatted properly for Kindle. After that you set the price for it to be sold at.

A great thing about this type of business is that it's really relatively quick. Once you hit the publish button your book will be live on Amazon for sale within twenty four to forty eight hours. When someone buys it Amazon will pay you a royalty and that money gets direct deposited into your bank account every month. Publishing your book as an audiobook can be done through the ACX website, just Google ACX and you will find it. Here you can add a new title by searching through Amazon for your book. Then you can either narrate the book or have someone do it for you. ACX really is becoming the pillar of publishing and we will talk about it in more detail later on.

When your book is live and published it's not enough to just have it up there on Amazon, you have to promote it and you have to market it. A lot of people forget this. They think that Amazon is going to do everything for them. There is so much competition continually entering the market that you have to be taking responsibility for the marketing and promotion in order to stand out. If you get traction on Amazon that's where you can get a huge compounding effect because they will promote your book for you and rank it high up in their search results. They'll recommend the book to other customers of theirs and then it can really take off.

There's a lot of books out there that are great books that nobody knows about and nobody buys them because a lot of authors unfortunately are really bad marketers. Marketing is one of the most important skills that will allow you to make money here but also this is a skillset that is transferable to any other business. There's a million ways that you can market your book online. The first way to utilize is Amazon because your book is published on there. Really there are two ways that you can market your book on Amazon. One is through Amazon search which is all about identifying the right keywords that you can rank your book for. You can outrank a lot of the competition fairly easily because a lot of the books on Amazon are not really marketing outside of it. This gives you a huge advantage to promote through external websites and social media. The next is PPC which is pay-per-click advertising on Amazon's platform. Amazon offer sponsored adverts so you can actually pay them and have your book show up on other people's book listings. It's a great way to get a boost because the more sales that you get then the better your books will rank on Amazon.

Amazon will fluctuate and change things that will be outside of your control but if you diversify your streams of traffic then you have an advantage. This way you can really blow up your business and build it into a sustainable one. Amazon want you to promote on social media, on your blog and other websites so that you're sending more customers to them. If you build your own lists of customers and build a relationship with them then it will be a lot easier for you to be able to sell to them. Then in turn if you can do that then Amazon will reward you and rank you a lot higher. Additionally, ACX also offer great rewards in the form of bounties when you send them new customers.

When it comes to traffic there's three different types, there's cold traffic, warm traffic and hot traffic. Cold traffic is when people don't even know who you are, warm is when they now know who you are or a little bit about yourself. Then hot traffic is when they're really engaged with you. It will be a lot easier to sell or promote something when you have that kind of relationship versus when they don't know you at all. That's why you want to build that relationship with people online because that will help you to succeed long term. It does take time to build an email list, a social media following and a fan base. But by building that trust it makes it so much easier to sell your products. Traffic sources you should consider are, Facebook, Instagram, Twitter and YouTube. Then there's a blog which is a great way of promoting because if you can rank in Google and people consume the content then they will naturally want to have more from you. Maybe they come across a great article or video by you and then see you have a book that's for sale. Also you definitely need to build a list. Email marketing is very powerful and we will look at it in more detail later.

Once you start making money from publishing you can publish more books if you want to. Looking at the big picture and really what's going to make this into a larger business is building a brand. A big mistake that a lot of people make is they're trying to build all these separate books and different niches that are all heading in different directions. The strategy that will work long-term is aligning all effort towards one goal. Then that way you're building a brand that's going to attract people to you that you can then funnel and sell your book to. There's many other ways you can make money from this and your brand can allow you to do that. Maybe you want to have your own events, sell affiliate products, coaching or other services. When you build up your brand you're leveraging the potential for more sources of income and that is coming from your own customers. Finally as you get more into the publishing business you can build it up and then eventually you can outsource it all.

Find A Profitable Niche

There's really two ways to get rich, one is trying to invent something brand new and write something that no one else has ever heard of before. There are people out there that get really wealthy and make a lot of money doing things that way but believe it or not it's less people than you might think. The easier way to get rich is to look at what's already selling on Amazon or Kindle or for any business and to just build a better version. When it comes to Kindle publishing the best formula for success is to look at what's already selling. Where is the market? Where is the demand? What are the problems that people are having in that market? Can you provide them with a solution or benefit? Because as a business or an entrepreneur you are essentially solving people's problems and offering them incentives at a profit. It's all about identifying their needs, demands and problems. Then providing a great solution.

Thoroughly research the market beforehand because how you position your book is going to be very important for each specific market. It has to resonate with a demographic and the consumer. One way you can do this is to look at the bestselling books and identify the consistent theme of what makes them sell. A great way of doing that is to look at the reviews of the competitors. Look at what the customers are saying. Read the good reviews and the bad reviews because that will tell you everything there. It will tell you whether or not there's a market, what the challenges are, what customers want more of and that will give you a great opportunity to be able to target that book to reach as many people as possible. You really want to get in the customers headspace because you can rank a book and get all the reviews and have a great cover and all that stuff but if it doesn't meet the demand of the market then obviously they're not going to buy it.

So how can you find out if a niche is going to be profitable? First of all you can analyze what's already selling on Amazon by looking at the Kindle bestseller lists. There's different bestseller lists for all kinds of categories and you can dive into these different categories. For example there is weight loss, fitness, self-development, romance, mystery, thriller and much more. Dive in and see what takes your interest the most. Amazon provides the rank of all books and products on their website. This allows you to see what's already selling and that can help you to identify profitable markets. You can see the consistency of what people are buying and that can help you to identify keywords and niches. If you identify certain keywords and phrases that people are searching for on Amazon what you'd want to do is type in that keyword and look at all the books that show up on the first page of results. The idea is to make sure they're selling and that it is of course profitable. Strategy and preparation is vital in your success not just with publishing but with any business out there. Taking the time to do that research, to prepare and strategize is very important.

Specifically you want to look at the Amazon best seller ranking. Every book on Amazon has what is called an Amazon bestseller ranking which will basically tell you how well that book is selling. Typically I like to find books that are selling above a hundred thousand ranking and that are around the $2.99 price range. If I can find a lot of books that are selling in that market within a hundred thousand ranking or better then that gives me the confidence and the certainty that there's a market here. Now you might be concerned about competition, but it is a great thing. Whenever I find a market where there's no competition I get worried and never ever publish in those markets. Competition is healthy and there are many ways you can stand out.

Incidentally you do want to make sure that those other competing books aren't too successful. If there are more than four books in the top ten thousand ranking then you wouldn't want to go into that niche as it would be very hard to compete. Unless your going to build a brand around it and position yourself as an authority in that niche it just isn't worth competing with those giants. Other things to look out for are saturation. Look at the publishing dates of each book on the first page of results. If there are more than four published within the last six months then you should avoid that niche as it is constantly being published in. At the start your book might do well but it will gradually be pushed down.

Follow this process through a few times and get yourself a bunch of keywords. Ideally if your starting out you want at least two niches to dive into. Save those searches in an excel or Google Sheets document. If you struggle to find any niches then check out hobby magazines, think of your own hobbies or check out the listings on wikipedia. You can also get some long tail keywords by entering text slowly into the Amazon search bar. It will auto populate and give you some more long tail keywords that can better fit your niche and narrow down the competition.

In summary, be sure that your keywords meet the following criteria.

Demand (four books on first page of Amazon within 100,000), **Competition** (no less than two books on first page of Amazon in top 10,000)
Newness (no more than four books on first page of Audible and Amazon published in the last four months).
Also make sure you aren't competing with major authors like Stephen King or Tony Robbins. Avoid niches with lots of reviews in them or with famous authors. You can use a great tool called KDP Spy to analyze pages of searches. Just subscribe and it installs into your Google Chrome Toolbar.

When you have a list of potential keywords you can move onto the next phase.

Researching for Audible

Audible is currently very lucrative to publish in. So many people are consuming books when they drive or multi task. This is really taking off and becoming the main source of publishing income. It pays to do due diligence and research on Audible. You can follow the above principals but then add in some extra research.

Head over to www.audible.com and start searching for your keywords. You should check for saturation that not too many books are being published there. Then you want to check for demand. Ideally your keyword should produce at least two to four pages of results. Avoid keywords that provide more than four pages of results or have thousands of reviews. In addition think about how your keyword would work as an audio book. For example books about gardening or cooking are unlikely to be valued as an audiobook. Essentially if you find keywords that have good demand on Amazon with low competition and high relevance on Audible then you have a winner.

When you search on Audible, look at the results and organize by bestselling. Can you improve on what the top four books are offering? Take a look at how many reviews are there. Can you get more? There is a great way to do this which we will look at later on in the reviews section. Take a look at all aspects, the cover, the title and description. Can you come up with something better? The title is really important on

Audible and you want to be confident that you can do a great job.

The Top Five Niches

To help you get started here are some of the most profitable niches.

Top Niche Number Six

Fiction books, many people say that fiction doesn't sell and that you need to be an expert. However if you look up the top selling niches on Audible then you will see that they are mostly fiction. The same is true for Amazon. Women love to read romance novels and guys enjoy a good story before bed. This is certainly something you can tap into with a good ghost writer or even with yourself as the writer. If you can find that hot topic or idea for a series of stories then you can build a great following and highly profitable books.

Top Niche Number Five

Language learning books. For example how to learn Spanish, how to learn French, etc. People are traveling so much these days and learning languages is really popular. If you present your content well then you can really start to scale things up into all of the different languages. In fact you can break it down into so many more sub niches. For example, French for beginners, French vocabulary, pimsleur French and so on. Of course it is a really competitive area with lots of companies leading the way. But a great way to build up that following is to promote outside of Amazon and brand yourself as a leader.

Top Niche Number Four

Diet books. People are very weight conscious these days and it has built a lucrative industry for people selling this information. You can go in so many different directions and sub niches with it. Weight loss, bulking, keto, vegetarian, and much more. As an audiobook or ebook the content is very valuable to readers and it is easy to write. There are thousands of different diets out there and you just have to tap into the one with enough demand and low competition.

Top Niche Number Three

Self-help, is massive. You can just go in so many directions with it like mindset, motivation, spirituality, happiness, self transformation and much more. Again it is all about finding that demand which of course is likely to be there and then finding low competition. This might be the hardest part because most of the authors here are authority figures with a huge following. But don't let that stop you, let it inspire you because you can also start to build a brand around a niche in this category.

Top Niche Number Two

Business, investing and money. This can be anything about entrepreneurship such as small business, investing, real estate, money management, personal finance and all that kind of stuff. The great thing about this niche is these are motivated people who regularly consume content and will always be on the lookout for new information that adds value. They are also likely to listen to audiobooks when they're going for a run or driving to work. Find that niche that is going to add the most value to them and be able to present it in a way that captivates your audience.

Top Niche Number One

Bundles. These aren't exactly a niche but they may as well be because they are very lucrative. When you have started to publish a few books you will probably have a few similar ones. The great thing you can do is to bundle them together into a new book. Then you can sell them again in all of the formats, audio, paperback and ebook. For the customer it is really valuable and for you, well your increasing your profits with little investment. They are really quick and easy to do and we will take a detailed look at them later on.

Write a Title That Sells

At this stage you should have some good keywords that you feel are profitable and interesting enough for you. For beginners I suggest you start with two keywords for two different books. Before you write the book you want to come up with a title, description, table of contents and the overall concept. This will allow you to have a better understanding of what your book is going to include. Let's take a look at the steps.

Step One: Competition

Choose where you want to focus your main sales to come from, is it going to be on Amazon, Audible or both? Right now ebooks are the least profitable, then you have paperbacks and audiobooks. Paperbacks you can push more with AMS and we will look at that later. Personally due to the massive profits and low competition I choose to focus on Audible. To get started you need to take a look at your competitors. Enter your chosen keyword into www.amazon.com or www.audible.com

Identify the four best sellers and paste the links and titles of them into a new document. You will be referring to these later on.

Step Two: Customer Research

Now when it comes to writing great titles and descriptions you want to write them to specifically appeal to your audience. Discuss their problems, desires and offer solutions or benefits in their style of language. There are some great resources you can utilize to tap directly into the minds of your target market.

2A. Researching Amazon

Search for your keyword.
- Go to the reviews area
- Note phrases and words that are unique to the niche
- Identify any problems or benefits relevant to the customers
- Copy these into your document

2B. Researching Forums

- Search your keyword into Google: keyword + forum
- Reddit
    - Look at most discussed and most viewed topics
- Take notes on relevant phrases, benefits and problems

2C. Researching Youtube

- Search for videos that use your keyword
- Look at the titles
- Listen to the vocabulary and topics discussed
- Take notes on specific phrases, benefits and problems

2D. Researching Successful Companies,
- How do they market?
- Take notes on certain phrases, benefits and problems

2E. Researching Udemy
- Find courses related to your keyword
- Look at the descriptions and titles, try to create something similar
- Look at the reviews
- Take notes on certain phrases, benefits and problems

Step Three: The Title

There are four proven great ways of writing titles and they are really easy to create. You can take all of your previous niche research and use it to fit into one of the four different title styles. I often find that some reviews even have great titles which you are free to use. I suggest you come up with at least three to four different types of titles from the four title styles. You will then have a good selection to choose from. When you decide on the final one go with what fits best within your niche. Remember to refer back to the top four competitors to ensure you are staying relevant.

Title Style 1: Curiosity
This title style is all about piquing interest through curiosity. In essence it will make you curious to find out more. It's kind of like a click-bait title.
Examples:

- *The Storytellers Secret*
- *The Road to Riches*
- *Too Good to Be True*

Title Style 2: Laziness/Shortcut
This style is all about presenting the book as something that will require minimal effort. Aimed at lazy people or those who don't have much time.
Examples:
- *Get Rich Quick*
- *The Fat Loss Shortcut*
- *Passive Income*

Title Style 3: Questions
This style is all about asking question aimed specifically at your customers. Use their language style and phrases.
- *Why are so many people getting rich with…?*
- *Did you know that athletes…?*
- *Do you want financial freedom?*

Title Style 4: Self Interest/Straight Benefit
This style is aimed specifically at a character of audience within your niche.
Examples:
- *How stay at home moms can lose weight without a gym*
- *how java developers…*
- *How traders always make money…*

When you have come up with a few titles in each of the styles ask yourself the following questions to come up with the perfect title.

Will this attract my ideal readership?
Make sure the title is aimed specifically at your audience. You should be using their language and resonating with their interests or problems. Will my target readership want to buy and read this book?

Does it incorporate my main keyword /keywords in a natural way?
Incorporating your main keyword into the title is essential. Audible will rank your book according the keywords in the title. It doesn't matter if you enter the keywords into the keyword submission of KDP. Therefore you need the keywords in the title or subtitle. But do it in a natural way and not just stuffed in there.

Is this title catchy, interesting, and compelling?
Again this is about being natural and tuned into your audience. It should captivate their interest and be so memorable and influence them to find out more or buy it. Imagine selling that book door to door, in two sentences what would you say?

Examples of bad titles:
The same as others, tricking people, lack of believability, keyword stuffing.

Avoid the above at all costs!

Now that you have come up with a title for your book, compare them against the four best sellers and also check again against the criteria. When you are happy to move forward you can get started on the cover.

Covers That Convert

Now that you have your title written it's time to get a cover designed. The cover is really important and you want to put plenty of thought and research into it before you have one made. There are some great options available for very reasonable prices or if want, you can design your own.

First of all go back to your keyword research and look at the first page of results. Take a look at the designs of the best sellers. What color scheme do they use? How are they placing their images and text? What is the theme, professional, fun, simple? To stand out you can use a contrasting color scheme. For example if they use red, use blue. If they use white, use black and so on. However if you are writing a book about a specific brand or company for example a book about YouTube or Facebook then you should consider using the color scheme of that brand.

Once you have come up with a specification you can start the design process. I suggest using www.fiverr.com For less than ten dollars you can get a professional design for your cover. Just search kindle cover or find the relevant category and look through the results. I usually filter results to be by best selling and then identify the ones with the best reviews and designs. Also look at their delivery times and if they offer revisions. You should go for multiple revisions if possible as its very likely that you will want changes. Delivery time is great if its within twenty four hours or even forty eight hours. Once I have a designer that I like, I will usually keep them for all of my later projects. When you have found one you like, send them your outline which will include color scheme, style, title and pen name. You can also link to some examples that you like. When it is delivered you may need revisions and that will be easy to do when you clearly instruct your designer. Alternatively you can design yourself. Adobe Spark and Photoshop are great tools for that. Just make sure you have cleared the copyright for any images you use. Also put your author name on there, normally this will be centered at the bottom.

ACX Cover

ACX/Audible use a different size to Kindle for their covers. Specifically it is more wide and square sized at 2400 x 2400 pixels. You can resize your Kindle cover to those dimensions but that isn't really going to look professional, avoid doing that. I encourage you to always have another similar cover made specially for Audible so that you are optimizing that part because it's really important. Some services on Fiverr will include that option which is great. You will also need to format your cover for the hard copy, print version of your book. Again you can find someone on Fiverr for this. Don't pay them more than five dollars and go for twenty four hour delivery for that service. More information on formatting later.

How to Write Book Descriptions That Sell

Now that you have your cover and title ready you can begin to write the book description. This is the text that will show up next to your book when it is viewed on Amazon or Audible. It is a really vital part of information that you can utilize to sell to your customers. Amazon allows upto to four thousand words for the description. But don't try to sell it too hard, instead focus on understanding your customers and resonating with them. Again you can keep things simple and relevant by using your customer research data.

Step One: Description Headline

Great descriptions begin with a description headline. This is going to utilize one of the title styles we discussed earlier. Curiosity, laziness and self interest. Choose one of them. Just look at what is popular in your niche and do something similar. For this you will probably have some left over titles from when you were deciding on those main titles earlier on.

Step Two: Book Description

The book description is where you are going to really, discuss problems and benefits of the subject matter using the language of your target market. You should start out with a couple of questions. Questions will set the frame and capture the customers attention. They should really be relevant to their wants, needs and pose you as being credible. Again you can use your research here. For example:

- *Are you a stay at home mom?*
- *Do you want to discover the secret to passive income?*
- *Would you like to get fit?*

Next you can move onto **if** and **then** statements. These would follow your questions. For example.

- *If you struggle with (customer problem or desire) then keep reading*
- *If you have always wanted to (common customer problem or desire) then read on*

Now you want to get into the process of discussing and stating facts about your niche and what your book is going to offer. This is the part where you are relating to your customers. Use statements such as **did you know,** then a fact about the niche. This is great if it is something that arouses a lot of interest. For example:

- *Did you know that most of the worlds best guitar players can't read music?*
- *Did you know that drinking coffee will help you lose fat?*
- *Did you know that ninety percent of millionaires dropped out of high school?*

You can also use synonyms, credibility and likeability factors. This is all about attaching yourself to already successful things or people and building trust in your book. In that regard your becoming an authority in your niche. For example:

- *This has the power to be the next Amazon*
- *It's so good that the top athletes swear by it*
- *Donald Trump uses this powerful habit everyday*

Add more into the description from your research. I like to choose the best parts that really paint a powerful description that taps into the minds of a customer. Continually draft your description and read it out aloud. It should read really smoothly, imagine you are pitching it to a customer. Does it flow naturally? Is it compelling, is it relevant and is it going to make them buy?

At the end you should put in some bullet points which will essentially be snippets of the best parts of your book but written in an intriguing way. It's almost like your giving out the best bits but not quite the whole thing, in essence saiting their taste. You can use the title methods here and also apply the credibility and likeability factors. In addition take some of the the best ideas out of the book. You can ask the ghost writer to highlight the best parts or do that as you write. Other things you can apply are, keep it mysterious. Use who, what where, when and how. Remove objection / common customer problem. Be counter intuitive / it can't be done. Don't do this, do that. Finally as an example it should look like this with about eight to twelve bullet points.

In this book (title) you will discover

- *The three most powerful words you can use when selling*
- *How to tell a compelling story*
- *Formatting tips that make your copy a joy to read*
- *Write an effective call to action*
- *How to write headlines that draw people in*
- *The technique used by olympic athletes*

Step Three: Call to Action

Finally at the end of the description is the call to action. This is your final instruction to the customer. Tell them what you want them to do (add to cart) Use **if** and **then** statements and highlight what action you want them to take. Remember to use their language style and phrases.

For example:
- *So if you're wanting to make your writing more effective and get a higher response rate then* **click add to cart**
- *So If you're looking to improve your chess skill and become a chessmaster then* **click add to cart**

Step Four: Formatting

When you have drafted your description and feel it's good to go be sure to have someone check over it. The last thing you want are any errors or grammatical mistakes in your description. Again read it out loud and make sure it flows seamlessly. To make you description even better you can utilize the special formatting tags that Amazon offers. This requires the use of HTML tags which you can use to make certain phrases, bold, italic or headlines to have more impact.

Typically you can start with a heading tag. There are six different levels of headings and also the bold tags which you can use to give more impact to your description. Highlight certain phrases or headings

HTML also has six different types of headings going from large to small. <h1>, <h2>, <h3>, <h4>, <h5>, and <h6>.
You can close these with the same code but use a slash /.
For example <h1>title</h1>

The bold tag is <b> and to close it is </b>

The <p> tag allows you to construct your description into new paragraphs. Each paragraph of text must go in between an open <p> and a close </p> tag.

Use the Italic tag to draw attention to different parts of the description. Italicized text should go in between an opening <i> and a closing </i> tag.

When you create a bulleted list use the list tags.

ul> Starts an unordered list <ol> Starts an ordered list <li> Sets a list item <dl> Starts a description list

To make it easy and see live changes you can paste your text into the following website and apply the HTML tags you want and then check how it all looks.

http://ablurb.github.io/

How to Write Your Book Super Fast

When it comes to writing the book there's really two ways of doing it. Number one is you could be the author, write your own books and do the publishing at the same time. If writing is your skill set, you enjoy it and you want to market them under your own name then there's completely nothing wrong with that.

Become The Writer

The task of writing a book for so many people is so intimidating that they end up continually putting it off and procrastinating. They get writer's block or they're not in the right headspace. Not that it actually takes a long time to write the book it's more so the procrastination and everything that happens with people putting off the writing that takes most time. In order to write a book speed of implementation is paramount. First of all there are a few things that have to happen for you to adopt this kind of mindset.

A lot of people when they think about writing a book imagine it as being a book that is must be hundreds of pages long. It's going to be this epic, high quality book with perfect grammar and spelling and it's going to take them at least a year to write. Now the interesting thing about ebooks is that less than ten percent of people who buy a book even read past the first chapter. Now why is it that people aren't reading these books? The main reason is because people are intimidated by the process of reading, especially if that book is more than one hundred pages long. They just end up procrastinating. You really don't need to write an epic sized book. Thirty thousand words is fine and that is only about sixty to eighty pages.

The average writer types around forty to sixty words per minute and a thirty thousand book can be written in ten hours or less. Start out by mapping out the chapters. Take a look at your competitors, what content is in their books? What are the main points of interest? Review your research and identify topics for chapters. Udemy is a great source of information in this regard. Incidentally you don't have to know anything about the topic that you're going to create a book on. Today everything is free and you can research anything online.

When you have your chapters and information sources ready, your halfway in. You can now begin to write the content. A technique that you can use that's really helped me is using a timer. This creates a sense of urgency and it makes you work more efficiently and quickly. Many times what happens is people end up surfing the net or they end up working aimlessly and they're not aware of the time passing. Set the time to write one of these chapters of your book within an hour. When your writing don't try to be a perfectionist because trying to be perfect is what stops people from following through. There's no such thing as being perfect. When you write quickly there's going to be spelling and grammatical errors but this is just going to be a first draft. Avoid filtering your thoughts and just let the words flow out. You're purposely trying to make sure that it's not perfect because when you have that perfectionism filter and you're micromanaging everything that you're writing then you're going to keep hitting backspace. Alternatively you can use a dictation software that will actually transcribe your words when your speaking. Or you can hire a transcriber to do that for you. At the end of one hour you are going to have a chapter finished in your book. It's not going to be perfect but that's okay because that's exactly what we didn't want. Now all you need to do is modify, proofread and revise it. Or you can have someone else proofread it and revise it for you. Primarily you want to make sure that you communicate your ideas in an efficient way, less is more.

Have Your Books Written Fast and Cheap

The second option to writing your books concerns focusing more on the publishing and marketing side. This is akin to the big publishing companies out there such as HarperCollins or Penguin. They're essentially a publishing company that works with different writers. In a lot of cases they work with ghostwriters or they maybe even buy, existing books already out there. They then own the rights to those and they will have a team in place to focus solely on the publishing and the marketing of the books. The benefit of hiring a ghostwriter is it allows you to make a lot more money because when you're the artist that becomes very time consuming. When you focus more on being the publishing company, then you're in a position where you can have a team and you can put more books out there and in turn scale up a lot faster.

When it comes to getting your books written for you and getting it done inexpensively there's a few things you need to know. Number one is you always have to make sure that your books are of the highest possible quality. A lot of people don't care about quality and instead they focus on the price. They want to get stuff done really cheap and often the result is that they're left with a really low quality book. When they publish it, maybe they make money in the short term but it's really just a matter of time before it is not profitable over the long term. Quality is the most important thing that you have to know in terms of making your book profitable. It doesn't have to be perfect, it doesn't have to be a Stephen King bestseller or whatever because you can always improve the book and make it better over time.

How do you get books written inexpensively? Well there's a number of options for this. If you hire someone from North America for example typically you are going to pay them a lot of money for writing a book. However it does depend on the writer, their credentials and all that sort of stuff. Every writer will charge different rates based on what they're worth. Some of the top New York Times bestselling authors have ghostwriters behind the scenes that charge over a hundred thousand dollars for them to write the book. But don't worry, you don't really need to have that level of book. Not unless you're an expert and you really want to brand yourself. A cost effective solution is to hire someone from overseas in countries such as the Philippines where for example you can find high-quality writers for a great price. Typically they will have studied English in university, have great writing skills, can research for you and produce a quality book relatively inexpensively. I suggest using a website called www.upwork.com where you can hire freelancers from all over the world. More on that later.

Personally I like to work with writing companies more than freelance writers because the companies have already spent the time to find and train their writers. Additionally they will edit, proofread and format your books specifically for Kindle. You will notice that they are more expensive but they will save you so much time otherwise spent posting a job, interviewing people and all that sort of stuff. The great thing when working with a company is that you can publish a lot more books. If you work with a company they might have one hundred or more writers working for them and so they can produce ten books in the same amount of time that one writer would write one book. Again it comes down to scaling and leveraging yourself and that's why I enjoy running more of a publishing company because it gives me the ability to do a lot more. For example as an analogy let's say that you're a contractor building a house. The worst way of doing it is by trying to do everything yourself.

Trying to create the architecture, lay the flooring, construct the roofing, wire the electricity, install the plumbing and all that stuff. There is a lot of work to building a house! The smarter contractor is the one that manages and oversees the project. He hires an electrician, a plumber, a roofer, someone to do the foundation, someone to do the drywall and all that sort of stuff for him. In turn it gives him the ability to build ten houses at once and scale up a lot faster because he's working smarter and not harder.

Specifications

The success of your results from getting a book written will be in direct proportion to how well you outline your book. Successful books are reliant on clear specifications. If you send a writing company a specification saying, hey I want a book about the keto diet with ten thousand words then you're not going to get back a very good book because your writer has hardly any direction. They have no idea what you want or don't want included. You should spend a lot of time on your outline and it should be least a thousand words. Your research will highlight the majority of this. The better you get at writing out lines, then the better results you will get from any writing company or freelancer.

The outline should include, book length, title, keywords, table of contents, description and anything else that you feel is important. For the book length, ideally it should be thirty thousand words (not including title, contents, etc). This is because one hour of an audio book is roughly nine thousand, three hundred words. Price wise a three hour book sells for significantly more than a one to two hour book. If your on a budget then go for at least ten thousand words which will get you a one hour book. Anything less than that is not worth it. Here is look at the pricing scheme of Audible books.

- Under 1 hour: under $7
- 1 - 3 hours: $7 - $10
- 3 - 5 hours: $10 - $20
- 5 - 10 hours: $15 - $25
- 10 - 20 hours: $20 - $30
- over 20 hours: $25 - 35

Writing Services

When it comes to writing services there are some great companies out there that have a wealth of experience with self publishing. Let's take a brief look at some of the best.

Epic Write

Epic Write is primarily a web article writing service but they also specialize in Kindle publishing. Currently they offer three packages, $0.80 per hundred words, $1 per hundred words and $1.20 per hundred words. I usually go with the most expensive one which is still only $1.20 per one hundred words and is of a higher quality. That's about one hundred and twenty dollars for a ten thousand word book. The price includes unlimited revisions, proofreading and it is written by a native English speaker. Delivery time is listed as seven days but in my experience that's actually going to take twenty to thirty days. However the book quality is actually very high, well written and captivating because they're being not rushed. For those on a tight budget or who are starting out I recommend Epic Write.

E-Writer Solutions (EWS)

EWS standard writing package costs $1.50 for one hundred words, so in a ten thousand word book it will cost you one hundred and fifty dollars. If it is a technical book you will need to pay a bit more since there is significantly more research required. The quality of these books are good and they claim to deliver within seven to ten days but be prepared for fifteen days at least. Once you get a good book delivered to you talk to their customer service and ask them who the writer is because you really would want them on your next project. This will give your books a strong identity which is great if your branding up in a niche. It's also going to save you time and hassle. EWS is great for more experienced publishers with a larger budget in their hands.

Urban Writers

Urban Writers market themselves as being dedicated to providing the best writing services on the market. They work with some of the best writers and talent in the industry that are passionate about writing great content. Their prices start out at $1.99 per one hundred words and they offer four different packages to suit any business needs. This includes a Fiction package costing $2.59 per one hundred words. Plus they also offer cover design and book description writing. If your looking to get into fiction or to have high quality books written then Urban Writers are a great choice. The prices are higher but if you are serious about publishing and really believe in your niche then having the highest quality possible is going to put you right at the top of your niche.

The Writing Summit

The Writing Summit have three packages available from $1.99 - $2.69 per hundred words. They promise to deliver high-quality, engaging content every time. Delivery time is usually around twenty one days whilst books over ten thousand words may have an extended delivery time. If you need any revisions that's all fine as long as it is reported within seven days of delivery. I have heard lots of good things about them with most people reporting great quality and excellent customer service. Many of these writing companies are in fact quite similar and the choice will rely on who is available or your budget.

Upwork

Upwork is a freelancing website where business owners post jobs and freelancers apply to them. In this case you would be posting adverts targeted at finding writers for your books. You can get some great deals here. Just post an advert with your criteria, budget and then review the applicants. A word of warning, be careful because plagiarism is rife here. To cover yourself, agree on payment in two installments with the last instalment to be released from Escrow after the book has passed the Amazon Copyright Detection system.

When you start to receive applicants a lot of people are going to say hey I can do this job for thirty dollars and other people will say I can do it for a thousand dollars. You will get many different offers and the great thing with Upwork is you can go through all of these options, interview them and look at their portfolios. Set up a video interview and ask them. How will they research your book and where will they get their material? Request that they send you some samples of their previous work. Do your due diligence to make sure that they're a high quality writer and that you will be happy with the quality of their work. When you are reviewing candidates another great thing is that you can see the previous jobs that they have worked. This includes their feedback and ratings which is really useful to know because you can analyze what they've done and what other people have said about them.

When you find a writer to work with you can negotiate the fee and contract. Set up some milestones to review the work step by step. Remember to pay in installments and protect yourself with Escrow payment. This will keep your money inside of Upwork and safe until you are happy to release it to them. I actually have something called a ghostwriter and agreement, this is something you can send to them to sign. It is an actual agreement saying that you own the rights of the book when it is completed. That's another measure of protection.

Whenever you work with freelancers you're going to have some good experiences and some bad experiences. Sometimes you hire a writer and they don't deliver on time or they aren't as reliable as you thought or maybe they have plagiarized which is something you have to be careful about. First and foremost you want to avoid and negate plagiarism at all costs. You will never get away with it and Amazon will punish you for it. If you write for yourself make sure that you use good references and have the experience necessary. Do not copy and paste from other sources. If you decide to have someone write it for you then there are a bunch of services you can use to protect yourself. First of all work with trusted writers.

When your book is ready you will want to ensure it is free from plagiarism. You can sign up for an account at Copyscape. Here you can purchase credits which are used to search for plagiarism in the text. The best way to do this is to go through the book paragraph by paragraph. Highlight various paragraphs and paste them into Copyscape. Essentially it will search through archives of published works and check them against your text. It really is a powerful and vital tool. You never ever want to be sending in plagiarised work because it can get you banned. Unfortunately you can't trust anyone in this business. So take the time to make the checks and then once all is clear and good you can move onto the formatting.

How to Format Your Book

Formatting your own book for Kindle can save you money, especially in the beginning when you're trying to keep your expenses as low as possible. Most writing companies who you are paying should include formatting the book for you. Alternatively you can find some great deals on Fiverr. However it is a relatively easy process and I believe it's something you should understand so you can have your books formatted your own way and start developing a personality around them.

Microsoft Word makes formatting really easy and quick to do. However you need to first be aware of some things that won't convert to the Kindle format. First of all, what you see in Microsoft Word does not equal what you see on a Kindle. For example in Microsoft Word you see an A4 page but this does not get translated one to one onto a Kindle file. The reason being is that there are many different Kindle e-readers. There's the Kindle paperwhite, the Kindle Fire and there is the Kindle app for reading on your smartphone or your iPad. Elements that are specific to the separate pages of Word such as headers, footers, borders and all that sort of stuff will not translate when you convert to Kindle so you've got to omit these.

Do not format using the Enter key because on the Kindle you might end up with a blank space in the middle of a page or at the beginning of a page. That's not really something you want. Instead what you've got to do is to use page breaks. Every page break that you insert puts the text on a new page even in every version of a Kindle e-reader. I highly advise that you use page breaks wherever the space is needed. Do not use any fancy fonts because if you use some sort of rare fonts then they will not be converted to the Kindle file. Do use an interactive table of contents in the beginning of your book especially for nonfiction books because readers might be inclined to just hop around different sections of your book. To create a clickable table of contents you can use the styles feature in Microsoft Word. All titles of each chapter should be styled as heading 1, subtitles styled as heading 2, 3 and so on. This will then be ordered as per se in the table of contents.

The recommended structure of a book starts with the title, subtitle and author's name. You can put this in a large font to really stand out and then the author name can be at the bottom in italic. For the following pages you can put in page breaks and in fact do this for every new page so you have clear breaks for the new sections. After the title you will have the copyright page with your disclaimer and legal information. Remember that you do not need to add your book cover to the book file because that will be added automatically. Next I like to add in links to and outserts from my other books. You can also put any offers you have here too. Then you would have your table of contents, a dedication and then a preface or prologue. Then it is onto the book itself, introduction, chapters, conclusion and so on.

The only other thing is to add a "click here to leave a review" at the end of the book. There you can add a direct hyperlink to the books page so that your viewers can simply click on the link and then go straight to your Amazon ebooks page to leave a review. Also you can add requests for reviews on every other chapter. Just write something like, how are you enjoying this book? Please share your thoughts with a review (link here).

Here are is an example of a book outline.

Title, Sub Title and Author Name

Copyright Notice
No part of this book may be reproduced or transmitted in any form whatsoever, electronic, or mechanical, including photocopying, recording, or by any information storage or retrieval system without expressed written, dated and signed permission from the author. All copyrights are reserved.

Disclaimer
Reasonable care has been taken to ensure that the information presented in this book is accurate. However, the reader should understand that the information provided does not constitute legal, medical or professional advice of any kind.

No Liability: this product is supplied "as is" and without warranties. All warranties, express or implied, are hereby disclaimed. Use of this product constitutes acceptance of the "No Liability" policy. If you do not agree with this policy, you are not permitted to use or distribute this product.

We shall not be liable for any losses or damages whatsoever (including, without limitation, consequential loss or damage) directly or indirectly arising from the use of this product.

Can I Ask a Quick Favor?
If you like this book, I would greatly appreciate if you could leave an honest review on Amazon.
Reviews are very important to us authors, and it only takes a minute to post.

Offer

Add your offer in here. This is where you can capture emails

Other Books By

Add in excerpts of your other books and link to them.

Content

Hyperlinked table of contents.

Book Contents

Your book matter.

Last Page

If you like this book, I would greatly appreciate if you could leave an honest review on Amazon.

Reviews are very important to us authors, and it only takes a minute to post.

Paperback Formatting

Createspace used to be the place to upload the paperback version of your book. Recently they have merged with KDP which makes things a whole lot easier to upload. The actual formatting of a paperback is a little bit more of an advanced task because you need to think about paper sizes, cover, spine design and back cover. In this case it's best to find someone on Fiverr to format the cover and book for you. Make sure you send them your files and also what you want written on the back cover. Usually I have the book description here and pen name. When the files are delivered you can create a paperback version next to your ebook version on KDP. This will take a while to upload and then you need to preview everything so make yourself a coffee and sit back.

How To Publish Your Book on KDP

Here we are, you should now have your book written plus a killer description, title and cover. It is time to upload it all to be sold on Amazon. The first thing you'll need is a KDP account. To begin, all you have to do is visit www.kdp.com and click the sign-up button. Select, "I'm a new customer." After you have done that you will need to enter some information such as your name, address and how you would like to get paid. In the majority of countries, you will be paid via monthly direct deposit. However in some countries you might have to get paid by check every month from KDP. Finally you will be asked for some tax information. The process is very easy and quick to do.

Once you have entered in all of the required information and signed up for an account you will be taken to the main KDP dashboard. Here you can access all of your books, sales data and advertising campaigns. Creating a new book is really straightforward, just click on the create new title button. Remember that before you submit your book to KDP that it is correctly formatted for Kindle. This includes making sure that the book cover has been formatted and also that the book description and any additional keywords or categories are prepared.

First things first you are going to enter the book title and it's subtitle. As an example the title of the book could be "weight lifting" and then the subtitle could be "how to get ripped". Your using some good keywords there and in a natural way. Before you confirm that listing you want to make sure that your title and subtitle is optimized for your niche. In order to get to the top of Amazon, you need to optimize every part of the listing. When you enter the description it is also very important. You can use the description that you created in the earlier chapter. When people click on your listing, that's going to be an important thing for them to see. It's going to determine whether or not they should buy your book, because the description is a reflection of the book. If the description is not good, then people are going to assume that your book isn't good.

Next you have the option to enter series or edition number. You can use the series area to add in a few keywords spaced with commas. For example. Health, fitness, weight lifting. They will appear on your listing in commas next to the title. Try not to stack too many here because you might get penalized by Amazon. If your publishing a second, third or other edition use the edition area to enter those details, otherwise leave it blank.

Following on is the book contributors which would be the author name. If there are multiple authors you can add them in here. Should you want to remain anonymous then you can use a pen name. Pen names are very common in the publishing industry. When your choosing a pen name take a look for any recurrent themes in the niche such as mostly female authors, foreign names, etc. The next part is to verify your publishing rights. You can select either this is public domain work or not public domain and that you own the rights to it. Next is choosing the categories for your book. You can choose up to two different categories. It's best to pick the most relevant categories for your book. Take a look at your competitors and what categories they are ranking in. You can also come back and change these later on if you need to optimize for more.

Keywords

Next up is the field where you can enter up to seven different keywords for your Kindle book. This is very important because Amazon is a search engine. People are searching for certain keywords. You want to find out what people are searching for so that you can rank your book for those keywords. Choose the most relevant, high demand and low competition keywords. Having different variations is important, because it can allow you to rank in totally different categories on Amazon which can help to increase your sales. To start you can use your keywords that were identified in the earlier chapter. At this stage you probably have just a couple. Ideally you want at least ten more because you can add up to seven for your listing then upto one hundred for AMS adverts. Here are five steps to find more keywords.

Step 1: Use your main keywords to search for relevant audiobooks on Audible. Look at the titles, subtitles and descriptions of the main/most relevant audiobooks on the first page of results. Are there any keywords that look relevant? Make a note of them.

Step 2: Slowly enter your keywords into Audible and let it auto populate the search field. Are there any keywords that look relevant? Make a note of them.
Step 2: Use your main keywords to search for books on Amazon. Look at the titles, subtitles and descriptions of the main/most relevant books on the first page of results. Are there any keywords that look relevant? Make a note of them.
Step 3: Slowly enter your keywords into Amazon and let it auto populate the search field. Are there any keywords that look relevant? Make a note of them.
Step 4: Enter your keywords into Google Trends and Google Keyword tools. Are there any keywords that look relevant? Make a note of them.
Step 5: Again enter all of the keywords into Amazon and Audible. Take note of the ones that get the most relevant, high demand and low competition results.

Categories

Amazon offers the choice of upto two categories for your books and you should choose categories that are most relevant to the niche and themes of your books. Later on you can also move around categories when the book is live and published. Those changes will take only a few hours as well. For example, if you find your book is selling really well you can move into a more difficult category and get more sales because more people will be looking at those popular categories. It's all about getting to the top of the most popular categories and achieving more organic sales.

At first, the best way to decide on categories is to look at the bestsellers in your niche and see what categories they are ranking in. Head over to Amazon and search for the most relevant keywords that describe your book. Find an example of a book that's similar and scroll down to the information about it's rank. Beneath that rank will be the categories that it is listed in. Find a couple more examples of books similar to yours that are selling well. Look at what categories they are listed in and when you find a pattern of similar categories amongst the top sellers then you can go with those categories.

In addition when your book is live you can actually get Amazon to add even more categories to your listing. In fact you can actually get them to show up for a total of ten categories. To do that go to the contact page of KDP and navigate to the help page. Select update information about a book. At this point they will offer to contact you by a phone number, input your phone number and then they're going to immediately contact you. When they call you just give them the ASIN number and what categories you want to be added. After getting off the phone your book will automatically show up with the new categories added.

Releasing Your Book

Following on from the categories is the book release option. If you want the book to be published immediately and your ready go then you can just leave it as, "I'm ready to release my book now." Alternatively if you you want to hype up the launch campaign and have your book on pre-order, then you can select, "Make my book available for pre-order." This is a great way to have your book launched with reviews and have other people check it out before it reaches the general public. All of these reviews and preselection will help rank it a lot higher on Amazon. You can even use some of those pre reviews in the editorial comments. When your ready you can click save and continue to go to the next page.

Cover upload, make sure that your book cover meets the KDP requirements. Double check the size, spacing, etc. Your designer should take care of all those specifications for you. Then you can just click on browse for an image, select and upload your cover file. Normally JPEG is the best format to use. Having the best cover possible is super important because it can literally make or break your book sales. Your book might be the best book, but if the marketing and presentation sucks then people aren't going to buy it.

Book upload, make sure that your book cover meets the KDP requirements. PDF or Microsoft Word Docs work best for book files. When your book has been uploaded you will be presented with two options to enable digital rights management (DRM) or to not enable it. Essentially this allows you to loan your book to other people for a period of time but if you want to stop that, then just disable it. Once you've decided on that, you can upload your book to KDP by clicking browse for the book file and then uploading it. When your book has successfully uploaded it will run spell check and notify you of any errors in the book. It will then give you the ability to preview your book to make sure that it looks the way you want it to. If a customer buys your book and it is difficult to read or it looks bad, then it could cause them to request a refund or write a negative review. Therefore you should always preview the book and make sure that you're happy with how it all looks. When everything is good to go you can, click on save and continue then move to the next page.

There's one more step before you publish the book which is to verify your publishing territories. You can actually choose whether you want your book to be available worldwide or if you want to target to individual territories. Coming down the page, you can select the pricing and the royalty options for your book. There are two different royalty options. One is a thirty five percent royalty and the other is a seventy five percent royalty. The thirty five percent royalty is only if you price your book anywhere from $0.99 to $2.99. The seventy percent royalty option is the sweet spot that you really want to take advantage of which is pricing anywhere from $2.99 and up. That's the primary price point that KDP wants you to sell your book at. Typically its best to launch your book at $0.99 in order to get a lot of sales and reviews. Once your book is ranked and it's selling at $0.99, you can then price it at $2.99 or more and raise the price to the seventy percent royalty option.

Coming down the page, you can choose to enroll the book in Kindle MatchBook, but that's only if you have a paperback version of the book live. If you have a paperback version, it basically means you can offer a discount if a customer buys both the Kindle and paperback version. You can also select the Kindle book lending library option to actually get paid if people lend your book. Once you're happy with everything and you have filled in all the information click on to agree to the terms. When your book is ready, click on save and publish and then that's it. Within twenty four to forty eight hours your book will be live on Amazon and ready for sale. KDP will send you an email to notify you when it is live. Then at that point, your book can start earning you money.

KDP Select

When entering your book details into KDP you will have the opportunity to join the KDP Select program. KDP Select is an optional program that you can enroll your books onto for up to ninety days if you choose to. During this period your books will be exclusive only to Amazon and that means you can't publish them anywhere else online. When that period is over you can then enroll your books elsewhere. I typically always enroll my books in KDP Select because they just offer so many incredible benefits that can really give you an advantage when you publish your book. However, after ninety days I take it off there and this allows me to publish it on other marketplaces. For that

I use www.draft2digital.com which distributes your books to Apple, Barnes and Noble and many other big publishers. You should really take full advantage of this and get your book in as many stores as possible.

During your ninety days on KDP Select you can take advantage of some great promotional tools such as the free promotion tool. Using this you can offer your book for free download for upto days which will help get you a lot of free downloads that will in turn rank your book much higher.

You can also utilize countdown deals to offer a limited time discount on your books. People react well to this kind of time restrained benefit. In addition KDP Select also allows you to enroll your book as part of the Kindle Unlimited Program and the Kindle Owner's Lending Library. Members of Kindle Unlimited will then be able to download your book for free and KDP will pay you based on how many pages of your book that customer reads. It's an entirely different payment platform that you can benefit from and reach much more of Amazon's customers with.

Paperback

When your book is live on Amazon your ready to publish the paperback version. This will show up in your listing as an alternative to buying the ebook. Try to do this all as quickly as possible. Actually the process is very similar to the previous one however there are a few differences. To start locate your ebook in your KDP account and then click the button to create a paperback version. Click that and follow the same steps as listed in the previous section. You can use the same keywords, categories, description and so on. Then click save and continue.

On the second page you will be required to decide on an ISBN. This is a unique identification number assigned to every paperback book. You can either pay for one or use the free KDP ISBN which is fine to use. Next you need to select print options. Now this part is really tricky so I suggest you find someone to set up your cover and manuscript for the paperback version. You can find these services on Fiverr for five dollars. They will take care of specifications and then let you know what the print settings are. Then you can simply upload the necessary cover and book files. Before you move on you will need to launch the previewer to make sure there are no errors. Your designer will help you to fix any if there are, make sure you have revisions available in your Fiverr order. Flip through the pages and see how everything looks and if everything looks good you can click approve.

Shown on the next page will be your printing costs and what territories you want the book to be available in. Personally I want my book to be in as many places as possible so I always save the default as "all territories". You can then set a price and it will show the royalty rate and how much it will cost to print. Normally I start out at $6.99 or more. If it sells well and I want to make more money I simply just increase the price. The next to thing do is to simply click publish your paperback book and then KDP will do their manual checks. If they do not find any issues it will automatically be live on Amazon and they will notify you by email.

Price Advice

What makes a book's price attractive enough that makes a person want to buy it? Is a book bought for its price or for its content? Remember that no price is final, with KDP the publishing is in our hands and thus pricing is also in our hands. That's why experimenting with various prices makes complete sense, until we find a price point that works both for us and for our readers. Choosing a price for an ebook to sell on Amazon through KDP has two ways: selling it for free, also known as perma free; and selling it for a price. There are some other terms and definitions we need to understand before we talk about royalty and pricing:

No.1 - Royalty plan - you either choose 35% or 70% - based on this choice, your final royalty earnings will be either more or less.
No.2 Primary marketplace - this is the base marketplace you choose for your book to sell. it could be amazon.com or amazon.uk or any other that you can choose from. There are thirteen marketplaces in total.
No.3. List price - this is the price you set for your ebook.

No.4. Delivery cost - delivery cost is based on the size of your ebook after conversion - the bigger the file size, the higher will be your delivery cost. No.5. Royalty amount - finally, the royalty earnings amount is calculated like this - your list price times royalty plan minus the delivery cost gives you the royalty earnings per sale.

Now that we have cleared out the definitions and terminologies, let's talk about some practical ways to price our books.

1. Perma free, selling for free has major benefits even though that sounds counter-intuitive. If earning some cash is not the motive, and you want to gain a solid following or an audience for your writings, go with this way. It does more good in the long-run. By default, there is no way to set the price of an ebook to $0. So, we choose a base price, let's say $0.99 and then publish it. We then also publish the book on other platforms, like smashwords, and then price match that in Amazon so they make it perma free. This strategy works wonders especially when your first book is part of a series and you want your first book to be free. But when it comes to free, here's an open secret with a word of caution: a reader has to have something invested in what he/she is reading and free doesn't accomplish that. Discount it deeply, but giving it away for free might have no value to the reader unless you are sure there is tremendous value in what you have written.

Next let's talk about some ways to sell for a price. KDP select - selling for a price, again, has two ways - choosing KDP select and going the regular pricing model. Let's see some differences in both: if you chose KDP select then your lock in period is for ninety days. If you didn't choose KDP select, you can opt in for it anytime. With KDP select, you cannot price your ebook below a certain price limit - for e.g. 2.99 USD or other limits based on your home currency. However with regular option, your lowest available option in terms of USD is just 0.99. For some countries like Japan, Brazil, Mexico, India, you have enroll in KDP select in order to get 70% royalty earnings. There are also some benefits during this ninety day period in KDP Select, which is that the book gets sold to the readers who have subscribed to Kindle Unlimited worldwide. Additionally, the book also gets more exposure through the Kindle Owner's Lending Library in the U.S., UK, Germany, France and Japan.

The only evident downside is that when you decide to enroll your book in KDP Select, you are committing to make the digital format your book available exclusively to KDP. During the ninety day period of exclusivity, you are not allowed to distribute the digital version of your book anywhere else, including your own website or blog. However if you want to distribute your book in it's paperback format, or in any format other than the digital format that is fine. There are some benefits to freely promoting your ebook for five days which is available when we choose KDP select. It could be consecutive or broken into five different days, the choice is yours. During these promo days, your book will be free to download, this is exactly when you send out newsletters to your audience. The more downloads, the better because that's when your book can even become a bestseller. Time your free promo days in such a way that it falls during the weekend days, and use all your five days at once.

As a concluding thought, practice smart marketing and price your books in accordance with what your genre dictates. Find out what other authors have priced similar books as yours. Then take it from there.

ACX

Audiobooks are the new core of publishing and a lot of publishers are missing out on this very lucrative opportunity right now. The fact is that nowadays many people prefer to listen to books whether it's on the way home, at the gym or whenever they have some free time. There are so many scenarios where you could listen to an audiobook and this trend has emerged with the multi-tasking nature of modern society. As a publisher you really do want to offer this option because it completes your listing for what you can offer readers and in turn offers you more sources of income.

Unlike every single other mainstream way of making money online there's actually a pretty high barrier of entry to be selling audiobooks. You have to get it narrated which is expensive and it's not as simple publishing an e-book for sale on KDP. However the demand is just as high as ebooks are and it's outgrowing them. There is this huge shift in the market right now from ebooks to audiobooks. At the same time the competition is really low. An ebook might have thousands of competitors but on Audible it might not even be in the hundreds. ACX was created in two thousand eleven but it wasn't until around two thousand thirteen when you could actually put your own audio files on there. It's only five years old which is crazy because as publishers we are very early at this wonderful opportunity.

To get started head on over to www.acx.com and sign in with your Amazon account. Make sure to use your Amazon author account and not your regular Amazon account or a different account. When you first sign into ACX it's simply going to ask you to enter your tax information and your bank information even if you've already done that through Amazon. It's not a big deal just go ahead and do it all over again.

To start publishing your audiobook you first need it to be live as an ebook on Amazon. Then you can click assert new titles and simply search for your book within the ACX dashboard. Once you've claimed your book it is going to show up inside rights not posted. It will present you with two options. Which are to find a narrator, or submit the audio files yourself. In most cases your going to be looking for someone to narrate the book so go with that option. Unless you are a trained narrator with great recording equipment it's simply better to outsource this and again leverage your time as the publisher. The agreement between you and the narrator is a pretty standard legal contract that you can go through if you like. After agreeing you will land on the next page where you can take a look at the details of your book. This section includes the description which is pulled from your book listing on Amazon. Check through it and make sure it is all correct. Titles are really important on Audible, you will be ranked based on the keywords in your title and subtitle. Next you're going to input your name / pen name for the copyright owner. The print copyright year (this year) and the audiobook copyright owner. Then you can choose which genre your book is and the best category for it. Next you can select your preferences for the kind of voice you're looking for. This could be male or female, old or young, language and if any accents. If you don't really care you can leave it, blank don't try to get super specific only because you're going to rule a lot of people out. Additional comments are just something for you to put such as, someone has to be really perky and sound upbeat because this is a chick flick, novel or something like that. Then you need to upload a short one page sample of the book that the narrator can read for the audition. Upload a word file here because it's going to make their life easier. The audition script should definitely be one to one and a half pages. It says you can do two to three pages but I've noticed the longer your script is the less people are likely to audition for it because they don't have a lot of time. They're auditioning for a ton of different things and you don't need three pages worth of data to determine whether or not you like them.

When the audition manuscript is done uploading we are good to go. The next page covers distribution. The first thing it wants to know is how many words are in your book. Type that in and it will calculate how long the book will be. Try to aim for books over three hours long so you can take advantage of Audible pricings. Next click I own the rights to my book around the world. Now scroll down the page and this is where it gets interesting. How will you pay the narrator? You have a couple of options here. The first option is a royalty share which means you won't pay any money upfront but you will share all sales 50/50 with the narrator. This is a risk free investment because it requires no investment. The second option you have is to keep all the royalties but you will have to pay the narrator to produce your audiobook. I always recommend you do that because already ACX take sixty percent of your sales and if you do a Royalty share you end up with only thirty percent. Make your narrator an offer starting at twenty five dollars or up per completed hour. Some narrators will cost more and you can negotiate that if you feel it's worth it. Keep in mind that quality always wins.

Next thing you want to decide is the type of distribution you want. This can be exclusive to Amazon or non-exclusive. With exclusive you'll collect forty percent of the royalties and with non-exclusive its twenty five percent. Amazon really are the king of audio books so it's best to stick with the exclusive option. Next make sure everything is correct and then click on "post to ACX". After a few days auditions will start to come in. You can listen to each one and decide on the best. When you find one that you like, make them an offer for an hourly rate. You will also need to specify when you expect the first fifteen minutes to be done by and when you want the whole project to be completed by. One week to ten days is plenty for the first fifteen minutes. A month is fine for the whole project. Send them the offer and set how long they have to accept it. Once they agree you can send them your manuscript and they can then get started on your book.

During narration you can message your narrator through ACX should they have any questions or should you have any questions and so on. First of all they're going to record the first fifteen minutes for you to review and then sign off on. It's really important that you check your account settings and make sure that your email is receiving notifications from ACX. If you don't check regularly and you miss those deadlines it is only you to blame if your book is late.

Now once you sign off on that fifteen minute check point they will record then give you the rest of the book. Upon completion they will submit it to you for your approval. Once you have approved it you can send it onto ACX for them to review which usually takes about two weeks. At this stage if you paid for production you also need to pay your narrator. Always pay through PayPal. Then make sure you have the cover ready. You cannot use the same cover for Audible that you are using for Kindle because the dimensions are different. Kindle is long and on Audible it is a squared, kind of like on a CD. I highly recommend against stretching your Kindle cover because that looks amateur. Ask your designer to make a new one or optimize it for ACX.

Bounty Program

One of the best offers on ACX is their bounty program. How this works is you are rewarded a bounty if someone who doesn't currently have an Audible account opens a new account and the first book they buy is yours. If they stick with Audible for sixty one days you will get a bounty which is usually for fifty dollars. That's a pretty good profit for one sale. Take full advantage of this and drop links to your Audible books in all of your books and also in all of your promotions.

Marketing and Promotion

When your book is available online it's time to start to promote and market it. Try to make sure you have all versions available before you start to seriously promote it. This includes audiobook, paperback and ebook. Successful marketing and promotion requires driving targeted traffic to your listing and that would mean people finding your books either organically or through paid advertising. Those are the two things you should work on in promotion and marketing of your books. When the traffic arrives at your listing you need to be able to convert it into sales and for that you need a good product listing. In publishing that equates to, a good book, cover, title, description and reviews.

In order for your book to rank as high as possible for your keyword you need people to search for it on Amazon using your keyword and then to actually buy it. This will cause Amazon to associate it with their search algorithm that this Kindle book is more related to those particular keywords. This is powerful in terms of ranking for keywords. Instead of sending people a link, tell them when they download it to find it using your keyword first. Also actually ask them to review your Kindle book. Reviews are a great way to bring credibility and social proof to your books. Now as you probably know Amazon checks reviews for your Kindle book and you want verified reviews meaning someone actually downloaded or purchased the book first before they review it. The best way to get reviews is just to ask for it. Find people that could actually benefit from your book. You can find groups, forums or Facebook groups whatever is out there. Give it away to them and then they're going to appreciate that. You can then follow up with them afterwards and just ask them for a review. But be careful not to get into doing too many review swaps or paying for reviews. Amazon are really strict about this and could end up banning your account. We will discuss how to get more reviews later on.

Give away your book for free by using the KDP select free promotion period. Why do you want to give away your Kindle book for free? Because the more people you give it away to and the more people that download it then the higher your book is going to rank in Amazon. Then if people get value from it and they post a review on it that's going to help promote it more.

Social Media Marketing

Social media is a great way to bring some additional traffic to your book and Amazon will reward you for that with in an increased exposure of your books. Let's take a brief look at some of the best sources.

Twitter

Twitter is a great way to build a following that converts to loyal customers. Set up your account and post regularly. Add value through your posts and communicate with your followers. You can search for your keywords on Twitter and relevant posts from users will appear. This is really useful since you can then comment on those posts and say something like, hey I have this book about that and right now it's free. Try to engage in conversations and develop relationships that convert. Avoid being spammy because people will have their guard up against that kind of behaviour.

Facebook

Set up a page and post regularly. Test out various paid adverts sent to your listing. Experiment with titles, images and text. You can check out Fiverr for some great services that help you with Facebook adverts that convert. Join Facebook groups specific to your niche. Just search for your keywords and groups will appear. These are not those garbage book promotion groups. Instead these are active niche Facebook groups within your niche. Try to be active in these consistently by posting and commenting on posts. You don't want to be looked at as just somebody who's out promoting their books. Now to do this it does require a lot of time but you can outsource that. You can create a whole separate pen name profile and use that profile to post in these groups. Then you can outsource it to somebody who's actively promoting the books and engaging with readers and building relationships inside those particular niche groups.

YouTube

Make a YouTube video to promote your Kindle book. YouTube is a very powerful search engine just like Amazon and Google. When people come to YouTube they're searching for different keywords or they're looking up stuff. If you have a video out there that's optimized for those keywords then people are going to find your YouTube video. The video should be optimized for your keywords or you can even do the video with the title of your Kindle book. You can go on websites like Fiverr and get people to do the video for you. The content could be you or so one else talking about your Kindle book or just giving away something related to it for free. It could be just talking about a few tips that are mentioned in the book. Then you can take that video and upload it to YouTube and optimize it for keywords and just basically get it out there and promote it. Just by getting it out there and having that it can really help you get more sales for your Kindle book.

Email Marketing

You need an email list for one simple reason, to take the customers from Amazon and make them yours. Then later you can market to them, sell other products to them and just communicate with them on your own without having to go through Amazon. To do this with Kindle publishing we use what's called a lead magnet or a free offer. Essentially it's a free offer that you're going to put inside inside your book that the customer receives when they give their email address.

What you give away for free honestly doesn't matter it just has to have enough value or perceived value for your customers to give up their email address for. I have used multiple things and tested multiple things in the in the past with my books and I tend to run with the one that collects the most emails. I've used other books that are currently selling on Amazon when a customer buys one of my books they actually get that book for free. I've used free PDF guides and I've purchased products that I'm able to use inside my book to give away for free as well. Use your imagination and figure out what's going to work best for your customers.

Now to set up the lead magnet it's a relatively simple process. Step one figure out what you want to offer your customers for free. Once you have that figured out then you want to create what's called a landing page or a squeeze page. You can set up a link inside your book that your customer will click on and there they have the option to enter their email address. To create squeeze pages, I use Aweber which handles all the email addresses and gives me some great looking squeeze pages. There are also some great free ones, just Google it. Once you have figured out your offer and made your squeeze page you're simply going to make a single page inside your book that has your offer in there. It's going to have a clickable link so your customer simply looks at it clicks the link and goes to the squeeze page then enters their email address. After that they get the free product downloaded directly to them and you get that precious email.

What you do with these emails is completely up to you, personally this is how I launch ebooks with organic reviews right off the bat. The email list helps generate sales right off the bat. You have to be collecting email addresses it's the best way to ensure long-term success in this business anyways. Email marketing can be profitable with the potential to sell high ticket and or continuity products either by affiliates or your own products. One of the best and most profitable ways to create a internet business is to have a continuity program and high ticket items. Using email you can frequently send your list to offers or products. We're not spamming people it's offering constant value.

I connect with my readers in my niche at least once a month. That email doesn't have to necessarily be about my book, it's just the topic of something around my particular niece or something that I think they'll be interested in. By doing that and connecting with them every so often they know I'm not just trying to sell them a book or ask them for reviews or whatever. Every single time I email them they're willing to open my email to take a look. Make sure you have some sort of strategy in place. Now this does take a bit of time and effort like anything remember you're not a kindle publisher you're an Internet marketer that is what your job is. The publishing is just a small portion of it. Learning to market and promote through email is like the essential skill to have when you're doing any online business. Take this opportunity and learn how to become a proper email marketer to increase your Kindle business.

Now where do you start? Well I subscribe to all my competitors newsletters, that's the first thing I do because I want to know what are they feeding their readers. By doing this I get to see how good or how bad they are at email marketing. I get to see what are their upcoming books that are coming out and other ideas that you can basically take from them and twist into your own style. You just have to find a way see what works best for your niche and for your customers. You can engage with them on social media and other platforms as well so I think once a month is is okay but maybe for you it might be twice a month maybe it might be once a week even who knows you just have to make sure whatever you're sending to them has some sort of value. Don't over complicate this process find simple things that you could send them based around your niche. Set it up on an autoresponder and you're good to go.

In the early stages of building an email list you are going to have to put in work without seeing any sort of immediate reward because you just don't have the numbers of people on there to make it profitable yet. A lot of publishers don't want to do that, instead they just want to keep on pumping out more and more books. On the other hand there are publishers with lists of thousands of people but they can't get any money from them because they don't engage with the people on there. You have to be thinking about what your end goal is for this email list instead of building a list for the sake of it. Because if you build a list without realising why you're doing it then you won't get people on that list who actually want what you're going to sell. A lot of times it will be freebie seekers that have zero desire of actually buying anything from you. If you don't pay any effort then it won't work because people will forget about you. You need to be actively building an engaging list.

If you neglect this and say I don't need to build up an email list and you just want to keep pumping out books of going through the boom-bust cycle of putting out books that's up to you. But there are some other things you can do with an email list which progress your income past certain levels. Relying on publishing books only means Amazon owns your customers so if they decide to ban your account tomorrow your earnings go to zero a month. If you're not getting any repeat customers you're not upselling your customers at all you're just selling one thing to one person at one time and obviously with that business model your income is limited.

Book Promotion Sites

Book promotion sites offer a giant list of emails or social media followers that are willing to read books. All you have to do is submit your books information for the promotion and they'll blast it out to their followers. Most of them won't charge you because when they do that they actually use an Amazon associate link which pays them a commission when someone buys something using it.

The general idea is that you want to contact the promotion sites two weeks before your planned promotions. Book promotion sites can help if done right. They aren't an end-all and they don't make you into a major money-making author but when done in conjunction with other things it can be one more way to help you have a stronger and better marketing plan. The volume of traffic they send to your listing is also quite huge and will help your books rank high up. Here are some recommended book promotion sites.

Buckbooks

Buckbooks is probably the best book promotion site for you to get onto. However you will need at least ten reviews before they will consider you. Although if you use their Archangel Ink book production services you will get listed for sure.
Note: if you have a second book they offer a discount of twenty five percent should you also promote that. The promotion service is only available every six months.

Booksbutterfly

Essentially with Booksbutterfly you pay them for downloads and this is probably one of the only sites to offer that. Of course this is going to rank you high and for ninety dollars you get around fifty downloads plus KU reads. It's really up to you, personally i would suggest focusing on organic downloads or those through paid AMS advertising.

BookBub

BookBub is one of the best book promotion sites but they are quite hard to get into. If you don't get listed at the very least make use of having an Author profile there and get people to follow you. In addition they have an awesome blog with tips and help.
https://insights.bookbub.com

Bknights

This is a fiverr gig and costs only five dollars. They will send you a boatload of traffic for that.

Reviews and Launching Your Book

Reviews are really important in the marketing of your book and will set you apart from the competition. The best reviews are organic reviews which means a customer actually bought your book and left a review because they liked or they hated it. Obviously you want good ones, so make sure your content is great. If it is of poor quality you will easily get many one star and two star reviews. To get organic five star reviews you have to put out a valuable book that people will love. For the best results, it should go above and beyond what they are expecting.

During your free promotion is the best time to get reviews. A word of warning, don't attempt to pay for reviews or try any review swapping. It might seem easy and that you can get away with it. But be warned Amazon are clued up on these practices and will penalize you or maybe even ban your account for such activity. Anway, first of all check that your book is live on Amazon through a normal, organic search (it doesn't matter whether it's on the first page or not at this stage). During the five day free period phase I would also advise the following activities. You can keep track of everything in a spreadsheet.

Twitter

Every day of the promotion search for relevant posts using your keywords. Comment on at least seven posts per day.

Facebook

Join five groups relevant to your keyword. Post and reply to people in groups at least five times a day during the free promotion period.

Instagram

Every day of the promotion search for relevant posts using your keywords
Comment on at least five posts per day of the free promotion period.

ACX reviews

To help you get more reviews on Audible you can utilize free ACX promo codes. When you've published your audiobook ACX will give you twenty five free US and twenty five free UK promo codes. To acquire these send ACX an email (support@acx.com) and request the codes. Once you have these codes, add them to a excel data sheet to keep track of them. You can then start sending them out as a free link to your audio book. Reach out to your following if you have one and to people that know you. You can actually have friends and family use the promo codes and leave you reviews, that's fine. Go to groups on Facebook and social media, find a subreddit that has to do with your niche. The goal is to generate reviews from the free codes. When you send them out tell people that there's only one week to use them. That way there's a sense of urgency, they'll download the audio book and hopefully listen to it within a reasonable amount of time and then leave a review. I actually will have a spreadsheet where I list all of the people whether it's their email address or user name depending on how I reached out to them, date sent and what the unique promo code they are using is. Then what I do is after two weeks of sending it to them is to email ACX and ask them which promo codes have not been used. Because if they haven't used it within two weeks then you can reuse it.

To further promote the free codes you can use a great audiobook promotion site called Audiobook Boom. The way it works is for ten dollars they will send out an email to their subscribers with a list of books in different genres that are free for that particular week. When someone requests a free code for your book they don't send them the free code, instead they send you a spreadsheet with the person's name and email address and whether they're from the US or the UK. It's great because then you get to personalize your emails to send them the promo codes, follow up and give them a hint to leave a review. In the future you can even link them to future audiobooks that your publishing. The chances of you getting a review is pretty good. Just make sure you send them out to people that are interested in your niche.

Sell More Books With AMS Ads

If your books aren't selling as much as you want them to or if you want to earn some extra cash from them, then you can make use of Amazon Marketing Services (AMS). This is a great way to get more exposure and sales for your book. The first thing that you need to do is to simply sign into your KDP account and once you are here, click on the promote and advertise tab located on any of your books that you want to promote. Click on this link and you will be taken to the dashboard of AMS.

Before you invest money into advertising you need to be aware that AMS ads work best for high quality books and that not all advertising campaigns will be profitable. Therefore if they aren't working as well as you expect, refer back to your book listings. If you publish a book on a keyword that simply is not profitable and you are using advertisement to promote it, then it simply won't sell well because it is a keyword that isn't profitable. However if you can't rank a book you can use AMS to help get the exposure that you want.

When you start a new campaign you will first be asked to select either product display adverts or sponsored products. Always go with sponsored products. For the campaign name choose whatever you want to see, usually the book name, format and anything else relevant is a good idea. For the average daily budget I always start with five dollars and run the campaign continuously starting from today. Five dollars a day isn't going to break the bank and if the campaign is profitable you can just leave it running.

For the select targeting type always go with manual targeting and for the default cost per click bid for suggested keywords I always start with twenty five cents per click. Incidentally I usually only spend around fifteen cents per click. However in the future if you feel like you're not getting enough clicks you can always raise the cost per click to maybe forty cents or even more. That way you will incur more clicks and it could give your book more exposure if that's what it needs

Next comes the keyword selection. When you are choosing these you should avoid using vague keywords. Your allowed upto one hundred in total. Typically I have around fifteen to thirty specific keywords which are written down from my research stages or if I find more here, then I also add them. I think that's a good number to start with but if you do have more really, specific keywords then add them. Next customize your adverts text line. You can write a short sentence here, something catchy that will make people want to buy it. Don't overthink this part, you can always use some text from your description and also split test different adverts. Once all that is done you can submit the campaign for review. It really is that easy to set this up. Wait a few hours then Amazon will review the campaign and email you when it is live.

Advertising Summary
- Select a book to advertise
- Start a manual campaign
- Set a five dollars per day, daily budget
- Set start date and for it to be continuous
- Choose some specific keywords and add them

- Set the price per click to start at 25 cents
- Write a short sentence about the book
- Submit the campaign for review

After your book advert has been accepted you should let it run for a while and then analyze how it is performing. I like to get at least twenty dollars of ad spend before I change anything because then you have enough data to actually analyze. If you spent only two or five dollars you're really not getting any valuable data from that so give it at least twenty dollars of ad spend before changing anything. When you know it's gotten some time to pull in some data you will want to look at the cost (acos) on the far right. This stands for advertising cost of sales and it's your ad spend divided by your total sales. If it's below fifty percent then keep this campaign running because it is profitable. But if it's above fifty percent, terminate it because that means it's unprofitable and you're spending more than you're making for those keywords. If you have some campaigns that are doing really well I would suggest increasing the daily budget. You could go up it ten dollars or more per day. There really is no reason not to because if its profitable and you keep raising it then the more money you will make back. Other metrics to consider are the number of impressions. This is the number of people that actually view the advertisement inside of Amazon. Then there are the number of clicks that it already got which is the cost per click (CPC). This is something that I actually don't pay much attention to because this is something that you can also set inside of your advertisement.

Monitor Your Campaigns

The best results come from continuous monitoring, optimizing, and general upkeep of your campaigns after they're setup. After weeks of working with the system, many authors find opportunities that weren't obvious when they first started. Plan on spending thirty minutes, three times per week to monitor and modify your campaigns as needed. The most seasoned AMS advertisers check their campaigns daily

A/B Testing Your AMS Ad Campaigns

A/B Testing is the process by which you have two identical campaigns running except you change **one** thing. The purpose is to see if your change improves your return on investment (ROI). The ultimate goal is to keep A/B test until you create AMS campaigns that earn the most returns.

Create an A/B Test

- Find the campaign you want to test in your AMS Dashboard.
- Click "Copy" to create a duplicate campaign where you can make the change you want to test.
- Change the campaign name to reflect the change you are making.
- Change your ad copy. It's ok to start with a small change to see if one small tweak can improve your ad.

Give your A/B test enough time to compete with the original ad and see if either has a higher number of clicks, impressions, average cost-per-click, and ACoS (Advertising Cost of Sale).

Most Worthwhile Things To Change:

Changing Ad Copy has been shown to increase the click-through rate more so than anything else. The better your click-through rate, the more relevant your book is perceived to be, and the more your ad is shown on Amazon for less.

Avoid These Common Mistakes

1. Publishers select keywords that **people are not searching for**
2. Publishers select keywords that are **very competitive**
3. Publishers **are not choosing enough** keywords
4. Publishers **confuse the KDP keyword rules** with AMS keyword rules

Make Even More Money With Bundles

Bundles can drastically improve the revenue of your business. If you have a series of books or books that are somewhat related to each other they can be combined into a singular composition that is called a bundle. Instead of having just one book you can bind them and now you have two, three or more books in one. Then you are able to put this book bundle up on on Kindle and ACX to be sold as a new book. In fact you can sell it at a higher price because it has more value inside of it. You can then market and promote it as you would do for a normal book. Oftentimes bundles do even better than the single books. People will perceive them as being of more value since they contain more content. They are really easy to do since you have the book content written all you have to do is pay for the formatting then a new intro and outro for the audio book.

To create a bundle, the first thing you need to do is select two or more books that you want to bundle together. Preferably bundle together interrelated books from the same niche or a similar one. Create a catchy and good sounding title that includes as many keywords as you can get in there naturally. Take a look on Amazon for some ideas, just search bundle in the Kindle store. Have a new cover designed for the bundle. Usually you can go with a cover that is a 3D style and shows the two books included. The cover must match exactly the title of the bundle because if there is any mismatch it will get rejected. Also don't put the word bundle in the title of on the cover of the paperback version. Amazon seem to take issue with this. However for the audio and ebook versions it is fine. Once you have decided on which books you want to bundle you then need to put them together into one manuscript. The manuscript should start out with the bundle title then go into the first book and then the second book. Put the main scripts together into one document and upload it to KDP along with the cover. Do the same for the paperback version after it has been formatted. In addition make sure you have a great description highlighting that you are offering the value of two books in one.

When it comes to getting the bundle on ACX things can get a little a little bit tricky. You will need new opening and closing credits recorded for every bundle specifying the title, author and narrator of the bundle. Get in contact with a narrator that you've worked with before, although it doesn't necessarily have to be them. In fact you can find a new narrator on Fiverr or ACX to record those for you. Just make sure it is in the same format as the book content, all should be mono. Usually I pay five dollars for that. Provide the narrator with all the information they need and that's the title, subtitle, author and the narrator's name plus the copyright date. After its recorded the next thing you're going to want to do is download the audio files of the books you're going to include in the bundle. To do that just locate each project and then go to the produce audio section. Here you can download each audio file of the books. Then go to the produce audio book section and locate the book that is listed on Amazon. Then select that you have the files ready. Now you're on the homepage for your bundle where you will need to upload the cover and start uploading the relevant audio files. Put the opening credits at the start and the closing credits at the end of the bundle. Then you need a final retail audio sample. Upload the best audio sample that you can pull from the book to really sell any potential customers on it. Then you click I'm done and your bundle goes into review. The great thing about bundles is not only do they sell well but the process goes really quickly. Way faster than having to produce from the beginning so you can pump these out fast.

Building a Brand

At the start of your publishing journey it's a good idea to experiment with various different niches. However in the long term you want to start to narrow in on your ideal niche. This should be the one that resonates most with you and of course is the most profitable. You can then start to publish other books in that niche that are similar to your first ones. It should all be under one pen name. In addition you can also branch out to selling other things relevant to your niche. Now that you have a fanbase you can upsell them to your courses, merchandise and so on. That can be a brand in which you have a congruent voice, style and theme. It's all about focusing in rather then spreading out. It is very important to have direction with your business not only do you want to have a tight and concise business plan but you want it to have a sense of direction. You want your readers to sense that your brand has direction. When somebody visits your author page after they've already enjoyed one of your books and they see that you have several books published on a certain topic they will be likely to buy more from you. Essentially you'll be giving your fans comfort by knowing that there will be more products coming from you.

Finding a profitable niche is the important thing in publishing but staying within that niche is also very important. Think of it like building a house, when you're building a house you want to build a solid foundation first. If you don't build a solid foundation you're setting up the rest of that house to collapse. Finding a profitable niche is pretty much like building a solid house that will last you for years. Then it's important to establish yourself as a brand, you want your brand to be tight, focused and to revolve around one topic. Now does that mean all of your books have to talk about the same exact thing? No it doesn't, what it does mean is that you need to stay in the same relevant area. There are thousands and thousands of different aspects and topics within any given subject that you can talk about. When you are choosing a profitable niche you start establishing yourself as the expert and your business model as you go along. This is the key to having a successful Kindle publishing business. Start looking at what some of the most successful books are doing. Look at the top-selling authors and start learning from their strategies.

Convert your readers into fans. Have the back end of your books optimized. This means including a link in the book to a squeeze page or to promote something on your website. Then you can start to communicate with your fanbase. The more people you get it out there too even though you're not making money from that well those people are going to receive content and value from you and then they're going to be more likely to check out your website, subscribe to your newsletter and start following you and potentially become a customer of yours.

Author Page

Setting up an Amazon author central account is essential for your books if you want to create any sort of authority and brand around your books. If you have an author page it'll bring up your picture, biography, all of your books and even your blog feed. This is a way for your readers to turn into fans because they get to know a little bit more about you, see your other work and choose whether or not they want to follow you. You're allowed to have up to three pen names per email address for your author central account. If you have more you can create a brand new author central account and you can do this as many times as you need to.

To get started head over to Amazon author central. Just Google "Amazon author central". You can then sign in with your Amazon author accounts username and password. Create your name and once you click continue Amazon's going to look for every book that was written by that particular name. Scroll through and find your books. Once you've done that click "this is me". If your book is not in the list you can search for it by title or ISBN. Now once you've clicked this is mine, Amazon will send you a confirmation email. If you have a publisher Amazon may contact your publisher as an additional measure to verify your identity which may take three to seven days. However while you wait it's important to start moving forward in creating your author page. This is where you can start to create that specific page where your fans can check out not only a little bit about you but also all of your books.

Inside the Amazon author central dashboard you can add a biography, pictures and you can even add your blog so every time you post a new article it will show up in your author central page. The first thing to create is the biography, this is where you want to come up with the story / background of your pen name. You have a minimum of one hundred characters and no HTML whatsoever so it's just plain text. When writing this, think of who your audience will be and how they are going to relate to you. This can be a made up character or company, it's all about telling a story that resonates with your audience. Save the biography and then you're good to go. Next you can upload photos. Again you could use your own or purchase some stock photos. Make sure they resonate with your audience and are high quality images. You can add up to eight photos and you can even add a video. This could be a video about you or your books. Adding something to each area is very simple, you just click on the respective link and enter the information that's required. You can also add events. Say for example your speaking somewhere or you've got something important that maybe your fans would care about. You can even customize your author page URL so you don't send this ugly code but instead it can be something very simple.

Once you've made your author page look the way that you want it to, it's important to start to add particular information for each one of your books. I'm talking about the editorial reviews all you have to do is click on the books tab and then click on the respective book that you want. You will see right at the top there's an option for you to edit your editorial review, it's just called reviews. The key thing to this though is making sure that you bold and use the italics as necessary. What I like to do is italicize any quotes that somebody gave me and then I also bold their name. If you're really good at what you're doing it's important to build connections with other authors and people above you so that you can then impress your potential customers by seeing somebody that they know and trust totally speaks well of you. That right there should immediately increase your sales conversions.

Your Book Not Selling?

Many publishers find that they will make money on their books in the short term but it doesn't last and it's because they are doing the bare minimum. If you're publishing a low quality book and doing the bare minimum to market it, well then you might make some money in the short term but it won't last over the long term. In this business and in fact any business you always have to take the long term more sustainable approach.

One common reason why this happens is people publish a book and they see that the other competing books all have ten Amazon reviews. So they think okay I better go and get ten reviews as well. Sure enough they do that and then it's basically the same as every other book out there. Meanwhile their competitors are promoting their books and they're getting more Amazon reviews and out ranking them. Everyday there are more ebooks that are entering into that market and because you only have the base level of reviews it will be very easy for anybody to compete with. The solution is to do more than everyone else. You want to stay one step ahead. If you see a market that has ten or twenty reviews you want to say okay this is a profitable market and I am going to do better than the competition. I am going to get more reviews. Yes it is more work, yes it's more challenging but it's worth it because you will have the dominant book in that market. You will outsell everyone else and other publishers won't be able to compete with you. The result will be a sustainable and profitable book over the long run. You have to be willing to do more than everyone else and put in the work. There's no such thing as over promoting your book. Don't be afraid to be overly aggressive in promoting and marketing your book because it will pay off and help you over the long run.

Another really important thing is quality. You can have your book at the top and it could sell for a while. But if it is a bad book then it will start receiving negative reviews. Then of course it will drop down in sales and that's not going to be profitable over the long term either. Focus on putting out quality books that people will really appreciate. When you first get a negative review it can feel like the world is going to come to an end but it's really all about perspective. Look at reviews for what they really are which is feedback on how you can improve your book. If you got a negative review granted sometimes someone might be leaving a negative review that isn't warranted. But in most cases I like to look at people as being positive and I believe that in general most people are leaving honest reviews. Maybe there is something in your book that's lacking and I encourage you to take the time to really look into the review and then look at your book and see if it is true. Maybe the negative review was about a bunch of spelling and grammar errors in your book. Well if it was, look at your book and check if it does have a lot of spelling and grammar errors. If they are telling the truth then it's something that you need to improve in your book. Remember to look at it as an opportunity.

Now I know you might be thinking, what do I do once I've gotten negative review and how can I fix it? Well you can't get rid of a negative review, unfortunately we can't just simply delete the review. But you can reply to the review and say hey I appreciate your feedback I'm constantly looking to work on and improve my books and I will take this as an opportunity to work on an improvement. By saying that other people who come across your book and see that response will be very impressed by the fact that the author reached out to somebody who left a negative review. A lot of people don't do that but what that shows is that you have the customers best interest at heart. One thing that most people are really worried about is getting scammed. When they see an author reaching out to somebody who left the negative review for them it shows that you really put your heart and soul into the book and that you really care about the outcome. This will make them more forgiving with some of the errors that you have in your book. Especially if you're going to improve it later on. In addition you can also let your readers handle negative reviews for you. If you connect with your readers through email, a website and social media then they are more likely to support you and counteract any negative reviews. Ask them what they like or don't like or what they want to see in your next book. Produce books that they want because then they will keep buying and reviewing your books. You need to grow those raving fans that will support you, protect you and stand up for your work.

Ultimately, even if your book does have good reviews you still need to focus on making it better because it is an asset. Keep improving that book and it can become a sustainable product. Once your book is ranked it has to keep selling to sustain itself at that position because if it stops selling Amazon's is not going to rank it at the top. They will only reward books that are selling. When you rank your book keeping it there is very important and really what that comes down to is a great listing. Title, cover, description, content and all of that stuff. If you have a book that doesn't really resonate with customers then people aren't going to keep buying it. Make sure that when you publish a book that you don't just neglect it. Most publishers move on to publishing more books and they're not paying attention to their books. That's the wrong mentality because again each book is an asset. It's just like the stock market, you've got to keep your an eye on your investments. Manually monitor and keep an eye on the sales. If they drop off then you need to put in more efforts into improving it or the marketing of it. This can really help you to stay on top. Monitor your books every week, every two weeks or every month. Then you can quickly take action to promote your book or get more Amazon reviews or do whatever is necessary just to keep it at the top.

If your books stop selling you can use this checklist

1) Check keyword profitability and if appropriate, change keyword.
2) Check competitors' covers and if appropriate, change yours.
3) Increase the amount of reviews.
4) Change your cover colour.
5) Change your title or description.
6) Add or improve the content.
7) Change categories

Conclusion

Kindle publishing is still one of the easiest and fastest ways to make money online especially if you don't have much tech skills. It's got a fairly fast learning curve compared to a lot of other businesses out there and then also it's not as complex. Amazon has hundreds of millions of customers at your disposal and if you put in the time, money and effort you can convert them to being your customers. Focus on building a sustainable income that will allow you to consistently make money in the long term. Don't think of it as a get rich quick scheme or anything like that because if you build it the right way this can become a transformational income stream for you. Maybe it allows you to quit your job or increase your income on the side.

Success comes from publishing quality books that are already in profitable niches. A lot of new authors think up this fantastic idea that they are interested in, their friends and family are interested in and so they publish a book on it and it doesn't sell. Your market is the customers on Amazon and it is not your friends and family. The key is to publish books that are proven to be selling well on Amazon. Then you know there is a market for you and you just have to mimic that model. Focus on building quality books that convert to sales and loyal customers. Certain books will flop but it is all learning about what works and what doesn't. You might get disillusioned and think I am spending all this money but this is business and you need to invest money to make money. Sometimes that requires publishing books that you are not completely sure are going to sell well. The first few books are going to suck but don't get paralyzed in thinking that you want your your first book to be this bestseller. Publishing more and more books is the fastest way to learn what actually works. The majority of businesses are not profitable for the first three to five years. Now publishing should not take that long and if it is you are probably doing something very wrong. Don't worry if your first book doesn't turn a profit within its first few months. Just keep going and publish a new book and the next one after that. Always keep a record of what you are doing and what your goals are. Update and review regularly. In the end your books are assets on Amazon that will be around for years so eventually they will turn a profit.

If you want to guarantee success in publishing then find a mentor who has the results that you want. It will be someone who can look at your business from a bird's-eye view and show you things that you cannot see yourself. A conversation with a coach or a mentor for just one hour can change your life. Where do you find a mentor? Well if you put a certain type of energy out into the world then it comes back to you. Set that goal and take action on it. If you're sitting in your room doing nothing, nothing's going to come to you. In an online business or in any business you're bound to make a load of mistakes. Having someone who's done it before will help save a lot of time. Surround yourself with people that have the results that you want and never be afraid of being the least successful. If you are the smartest in the room then you are in the wrong room. Make friends in the business and grow with them. Start having weekly calls with them. Join groups and connect with the people in there, share with them and talk to them frequently. All of your incomes will increase and it will increase significantly faster than doing it on your own.

I wish you all the best!

William Swain

Thanks for Reading!

What did you think of, **The Ultimate Guide to Make Money Online: Build a Passive Income Fortune with Kindle Publishing, Amazon FBA, Affiliate Marketing, Dropshipping, YouTube, Udemy, Blogging, Shopify and much more**

I know you could have picked any number of books to read, but you picked this book and for that I am extremely grateful.

I hope that it added at value and quality to your everyday life. If so, it would be really nice if you could share this book with your friends and family by posting to Facebook and Twitter.

If you enjoyed this book and found some benefit in reading this, I'd like to hear from you and hope that you could take some time to post a review. Your feedback and support will help this author to greatly improve his writing craft for future projects and make this book even better.

I want you, the reader, to know that your review is very important and so, if you'd like to leave a review, all you have to do is click here and away you go. I wish you all the best in your future success!

Thank you and good luck!

**Max Lane
2019**

How You Can Go From Zero To $1,000/Month In The Next 30 Days...

https://www.subscribepage.com/makemoneyonline1

www.ingramcontent.com/pod-product-compliance
Lightning Source LLC
LaVergne TN
LVHW091046100526
838202LV00077B/3050